a Consumer Publication

COPING
WITH
DISABLEMENT

Consumers' Association
publishers of **Which?**
14 Buckingham Street
London WC2N 6DS

a Consumer Publication

edited by   Edith Rudinger

published by   Consumers' Association
publishers of **Which?**

Consumer Publications are
available from Consumers'
Association, and from
booksellers.
Details of other
Consumer Publications
are given at the end of this
book.

© Consumers' Association March 1974
amended reprint September 1974
revised edition September 1976
ISBN 0 85202 120 8

 *Computer type-set and
printed Offset-Litho by Page Bros (Norwich) Ltd.*

Many disabled people and elderly people need help to overcome problems of daily living. Most difficulties are not unique, and the same problems occur again and again. This book covers the common areas of difficulty and offers some of the more usual solutions, including alternative methods of doing things and the use of special aids. The aids market is small and constantly changing: what is available now may not be made in six months' time, but new ideas may have been developed.

The book does not attempt to offer solutions to the emotional and psychological aspects of becoming disabled, nor does it deal with the special problems of mothers and children or with employment.

Coping with disablement was written for the Consumers' Association by Peggy Jay, MBAOT, SROT. In the course of its preparation, CA consulted, amongst others, occupational therapists, physiotherapists, doctors, designers, disabled consumers, local authority officers, the DHSS, voluntary organisations, and had the advice and help of the information officer of the Disabled Living Foundation.

CONTENTS

Many handicapped, and for that matter ablebodied, people put up with practical difficulties in everyday living that need not exist. There is no merit in doing things the hard way. Usually, successful adjustment is made by thinking out the problems and then being able to look for solutions.

Most commonly the major problems are getting about, both inside and outside the house; problems of reaching down to the feet or up to a cupboard; problems of limited strength and loss of stamina. Someone who is disabled or elderly gets fatigued quickly and therefore it is important to find easier and less tiring ways of doing things. When someone has limited capacity, it is probably better to get help with the activities that are most exhausting and to do the things most enjoyed and most easily managed.

To overcome a practical problem, different people require different levels of assistance. Some can manage on their own if taught how; others can be helped easily by another person if they learn how help should be given and accepted; yet others can manage only with a mechanical aid, and some may even need help to use this.

An aid is not necessarily the solution. To learn an alternative method is nearly always a more satisfactory way of achieving independence. A therapist will be able to assess the situation, will use her experience to provide simple answers to common problems and her knowledge of medical conditions to deal with the more complex ones.

Someone who does need an aid must learn the proper way to use it. The family also must understand the way aids and adaptations should be used so that they can make sure an aid is being used correctly and safely. Not using an aid properly or getting the wrong aid is a waste of money, whether you pay for it or the local authority or the national health service.

Not only is it important to have the right aid and be taught how to get the most out of it but it may take quite a lot of practice to get efficient at using it. Do not buy or accept an aid without trying it out first if at all possible. The simplest aid is often the best.

Even if financial help is not required, it is worth getting advice on aids, adaptations and services from people who have dealt with similar problems before and know what is available.

In March 1974, the government appointed a parliamentary under-secretary with responsibility for the disabled within the Department of Health and Social Security.

There are three main sources of practical help for disabled people and the elderly: the local authority social services department, the national health service which includes hospital services and community health, and various voluntary organisations.

The local authority
Local authorities provide services for both the elderly and the disabled through the social services department. There is much unevenness in the help provided by different local authorities. One authority may empower its social services department to spend up to £500 on adapting a disabled person's house before seeking committee approval, another limits such expenditure to £75. Where one authority applies stringent means tests, another may provide aids and services free. The frequency of meals-on-wheels deliveries and the number of hours a home help can give vary widely. The number of day centres where elderly and disabled people can go to get out of the house for a while differs from area to area, and so does the quality of what is provided: some centres provide little constructive activity, others try to help individuals make the best use of their residual ability.

It is unsatisfactory that disabled and elderly people receive help not so much according to their needs but according to where they live and who is dealing with their case. Local authorities have been doing better in providing help and services; members of an ill-served community should agitate for improvement there.

Local authorities have considerable autonomy in the way they spend their money (which comes from the rates and from the central government rate support grants) and are expected to know the priorities in their own area. The social services have to compete with housing, with education and with many other services for a share of this money, and their own services have to cover many other groups as well as the disabled and the elderly.

social services department

The social services departments are a function of the county or metropolitan district councils, each with a director of social services and a social services committee. The counties are divided into district councils and the social services departments into divisions of roughly the same geographical areas. These divisions are in charge of divisional directors, who have social work teams serving the needs of people in different localities in the district. Similarly, in London the boroughs have their social services departments.

If an elderly or disabled person, or a relative, needs any of the services of the department, they should call at the office of the divisional director, or an area office if there is one. The address and telephone number may be obtained from the social services department which is listed in the telephone directory under the name of the local authority. It can also be obtained from the local post office, the public library, the town hall or council offices, or a citizens' advice bureau.

When a disabled person receives help from the social services department, he is put on the register of handicapped persons kept by the department. There is no formal assessment procedure: the qualification for being on the register is a substantial and permanent handicap. Consequently someone who is temporarily handicapped, perhaps with a broken leg, or who is not considered substantially handicapped may not be eligible for some of the services provided for the disabled in his area. Being on the register as a handicapped person should not be regarded as a badge of disability but as an indication that you are entitled to a variety of benefits as of right, such as a rent rebate. It is an administrative matter which may authorise the expenditure of money on aids and adaptations, and helps the local authority to estimate what facilities should be provided for disabled people over the next few years. Under the Chronically Sick and Disabled Persons Act 1970, local authorities were required to discover the numbers and needs of substantially and permanently handicapped people in their area so that plans could be made for developing services for them.

—the social work team

A social worker is usually the person who first makes contact with the individual who is in need of help. The main task of the social workers employed by the social services department is to identify problems and either help to overcome them or help the person to come to terms with them. Some problems the social worker can deal with direct, such as arranging for meals-on-wheels or a home help. With other problems, the social worker will arrange for a colleague, for example, a geriatric visitor or an occupational therapist to visit the person. Social workers act as a liaison between someone in need of help and the statutory and voluntary bodies providing that help. They can advise on financial matters, including getting help to pay for aids and adaptations. A social worker can give support to the person concerned and the family, and help with the emotional situations they may face in adjusting to disability or increasing age.

Many social services departments will deal only with crisis situations and when the immediate help has been given, nothing further is done. This is partly a result of the current shortage of social workers. However, some social services departments keep an 'at risk' register so that their social workers can still keep contact with the disabled or elderly people they have helped, even if this only means visiting them twice a year, preventing further crises that might otherwise occur.

Increasingly, local authorities are attaching occupational therapists in an advisory capacity to social work teams. Their role is to assess the individual needs of the physically disabled in relation to personal independence, employment and recreation. In some places, they supervise work centres for the disabled or organise a supply of work for disabled people to do at home. Domiciliary occupational therapists visit disabled and elderly people at home to advise on any aids and adaptations needed there to help overcome problems of daily living. You should be able to find out from the local social services department whether an occupational therapist is available in your area and, if so, how to get in touch with her. In an area where there is no domiciliary occupational therapist, a disabled or elderly person who needs advice on practical problems should ask his general practitioner to refer him to the nearest hospital with an occupational therapy department.

aids and adaptations

Social services departments have the duty to provide aids where these are needed. The commonest aids supplied by social services departments are bath and lavatory aids, but dressing aids, cooking aids and indeed most of the aids mentioned in this book, come within their compass. Some social services departments provide aids free, others expect the person to contribute some or all of the cost. When it is difficult for someone to pay, they may get the money from voluntary or charitable organisations. Social services departments supply aids direct; they do not refund the cost of an aid the individual has bought himself.

In all possible cases, an occupational therapist should assess the need before an aid is supplied. Social workers issue many aids, such as bath seats, but are not qualified by their training to assess functional disability and are therefore not always able to choose the most suitable aid for an individual, and are not in a position to teach someone how to use an aid.

Social services departments are also empowered to carry out adaptations to the home. These may range from moving a light switch or installing handrails to putting in a ramp or knocking down the wall between the existing bathroom and lavatory.

When the house is owned by the council, the social services department liaises with the housing department. When the house is rented, the landlord's permission for any alterations must be obtained. In this situation, the local authority is unlikely to do anything major, such as putting in a lavatory which would benefit the landlord, but may help with minor adaptations, such as handrails.

Some social services departments are generous with help for house adaptations. Others try to raise money from outside sources for someone who has limited financial means. Yet others have neither the experience to give advice nor are they willing to help with money.

If someone needs a downstairs bathroom or lavatory or there is not one already in the house, a grant to put one in (incorporating an access door wide enough to take a wheelchair if necessary) can be applied for through the housing department of the local authority.

The financing of adaptations is only part of the problem. The major difficulty is to get the work done. In some areas, adaptations to council-owned property must be done by or through the council. With a privately-owned house, adaptations approved by the social services department may have to go out to tender, and since builders dislike doing small jobs, this can take many months.

A few local authorities employ their own technicians to do special adaptation work. These men work closely with the occupational therapists and many become experts in common adaptations such as rails and ramps. In some cases, the technician from the hospital occupational therapy department will do the job and the social services department pay for the materials used.

The department of architecture of the Cheshire County Council has produced an illustrated handbook, *Made to measure,* describing domestic extensions and adaptations for handicapped persons carried out in Cheshire.

day centres

Many local authorities recognise that it is part of the normal pattern of living to leave the house for at least part of the day and go out and mix with other people. Therefore, in addition to attempting to make life at home easier and more comfortable for disabled or elderly people, they make provision for at least some of them to go out during the day to some kind of special centre. This also gives some respite to relatives which helps to hold the family together.

Some people can attend a day centre every day, others on some days of the week, others for part of a day. Some centres are for the elderly only, some for disabled elderly people, some for disabled people of all ages and some for the younger disabled. Lunch is usually provided, or there may be cooking facilities. In some areas, there is transport for those who need it. Day centres may be run by the local authority or by a voluntary body. Information about what is available in any area can be obtained from the local social services department.

Day centres vary in what they offer. Some organise activities which allow the people attending the centre to make a small amount of money by carrying out light industrial work, or services such as printing or chair caning, or handicrafts that can be sold such as stool seating or toy making. Some day centres have a wide and varied programme of social activities, and people are encouraged to join in those activities that particularly interest them. In others, people spend more time sitting in armchairs watching television or playing cards.

Some centres use cooking as an activity. This should give an opportunity for someone who has had a stroke or severe arthritis to learn about the various aids available. It should also give a woman who for the first time is catering just for herself, or a man who has never had to cook before, ideas about planning inexpensive and easy but nutritious meals for one person.

Some local authority day centres have facilities for assessing the problems of disabled and elderly people. These facilities may include a kitchen, bedroom and bathroom where an occupational therapist can help someone to try out the various activities he finds difficult, and if necessary to practise with the appropriate aids. This should be followed up by the therapist visiting the person's home.

A chiropody service, a visiting hairdresser and perhaps an opportunity to have a bath with someone nearby to help may also be available at a day centre.

other local authority help

The social services department is responsible for the home help service, and for the meals-on-wheels service in the area. Some run lunch clubs. A telephone, a television set or a radio may be provided in some cases. Some local authorities provide a visiting library service for housebound people; in some areas, this service includes cassettes or records. Some local authorities help with holidays for the disabled and elderly, by providing holiday accommodation or subsidising holidays that have been arranged privately.

The social services department has information about concessions offered locally, such as free or reduced fares, special arrangements for shopping, outings, reduced charges for entertainments or services.

If a person's handicap makes it difficult to get out to vote at an election, it is possible to arrange a vote by post or by proxy. Enquiries should be made to the electoral registration officer.

financial help
A social worker from the social services department can be asked for advice on possible entitlement to financial help from the local authority or the Department of Health and Social Security, and if so, what to do. The DHSS issues a booklet *Help for handicapped people* (HB 1), available from social services departments and social security offices and citizens' advice bureaux.

Someone (other than a married woman) who because of disability has not been able to work and make national insurance contributions can claim a non-contributory invalidity pension. The DHSS leaflet NI 210 contains details and an application form.

There is an attendance allowance which is given under certain specific circumstances to someone who needs another person to look after him during the day or the night, or needs constant attendance (leaflet NI 205 gives details). A man or a single woman who cannot go out to work because of looking after a relative who is in receipt of an attendance allowance can claim an invalid care allowance (leaflet NI 212 gives details). An allowance for extra heating may be paid by the Supplementary Benefits Commission to someone whose mobility is restricted by chronic ill health or by general frailty and old age.

The needs allowance for a rent rebate or rate rebate is higher for someone who is on the local authority's register of handicapped people. A booklet *Housing grants and allowances for disabled people* (25p), available from the Central Council for the Disabled (34 Eccleston Square, London SW1V 1PE), includes information about improvement grants, adaptations, rent rebates and allowances, rate rebates and exemptions, supplementary heating allowances.

National health service
The national health service is administered in regions divided into area health authorities. Each area is roughly the equivalent of a local authority (county council) and also is subdivided into districts.

Medical and nursing services for the elderly and disabled in their own homes, such as a home nurse or a health visitor, are the responsibility of the health authority and are provided through the recommendation of the general practitioner. The doctor or the district nursing sister can also be asked to arrange for nursing aids in the home. If an elderly or disabled person returning from hospital is in need of care at home, the link with the local authority social worker will be made by the ward sister, a therapist or social worker of the hospital. Rehabilitation and the aftercare of patients discharged from hospital, which includes physiotherapy and occupational therapy, comes under the area health authority. The treatment facilities vary widely in different parts of the country.

physiotherapy and occupational therapy
Many disabled and elderly people attending hospital for routine treatment receive therapy to help with the activities of daily living. But many patients are discharged from hospital without this help. Sometimes this is due to the rapid turnover of beds; by the time the patient is well enough to attend for occupational therapy, he is sent home. People who are taken ill at home—for example, with a stroke—may never go into hospital and may, unnecessarily, remain dependent on their family in such basic essentials as moving about and dressing.

If it becomes apparent that an elderly person or someone with a disability is not managing to cope in terms of physical function or morale, the general practitioner can be asked if hospital treatment would help. He may then ask the appropriate consultant in the local hospital to see the person and assess the need. It is better to seek help early because the longer someone stays dependent, the harder it is to regain independence. Usually treatment is given as an outpatient, but sometimes inpatient treatment is more effective because travelling to hospital can be tiring. Living in a hospital or special unit makes it easier to practise, for example, independent dressing. Seeing what other patients achieve can act as a stimulus.

The physiotherapist aims to give you improved function by producing a few more degrees of movement in a hip, a little more strength in the shoulders or a little more confidence by making you practise a manoeuvre under supervision. Improved function is only maintained by use, and it is the occupational therapist's job to encourage this.

In most hospitals with an OT department there is a unit for activities of daily living (ADL), sometimes called a functional assessment unit. This usually consists of a bedroom, bathroom, kitchen and a selection of aids. Here it is possible for the disabled or elderly person to work with the occupational therapist to solve individual problems. Cooking, housework and laundry can all be practised under supervision; different bath seats can be tried in the bath, different raises on the lavatory seat. As a result, it may be found that there is no need for an aid. In cases where an aid is provided, the person has to learn how to use it; the physiotherapist may help, especially when there are difficulties of transferring body weight.

Sometimes the occupational therapist, perhaps with the physiotherpist, makes a visit to the person's house in order to look at the height of the bed, the width of the doorways, the need for rails.

—aids and appliances

Aids to mobility, such as crutches, walking sticks and walking frames, are loaned to patients by the physiotherapy department of the hospital. Wheelchairs are issued by the nearest Department of Health and Social Security appliance centre on the recommendation of a doctor. (When no longer needed, a wheelchair should be returned to the centre, not to the hospital.) Domestic aids, such as a bath seat or raised lavatory seat, may be lent by the hospital OT department or the occupational therapist may ask the social services department to supply what is required. When an aid supplied is no longer required, it should be returned to the local authority or the hospital it came from.

rehabilitation centres and other special centres

There are a number of medical rehabilitation centres around the country where a disabled person can get intensive treatment from 9 am to 5 pm, five days a week. Many people improve their functional ability more quickly under this regime than attending hospital for a few hours a few days a week. Such centres cater mainly for younger disabled people who have had a road accident or an industrial accident, or who have, for instance, parkinsonism, multiple sclerosis, hemiplegia. Most of the centres are residential.

There are some special centres in the country for treating people with severe disabilities, such as head injuries. There are also spinal injury units, and assessment centres, such as Mary Marlborough Lodge at Oxford which specialises in assessing the very severely disabled who may need sophisticated aids and appliances. Patients are referred to these centres by either their general practitioner or a hospital consultant. The social worker in the hospital may also know of them.

geriatric units
Some hospitals with a geriatric unit will admit an elderly person who is normally cared for at home, for short periods. This gives the doctors and therapists a chance to do a check-up on the old person and deal with any problems that may have arisen. It also gives relatives a rest and may be an important factor in enabling them to continue to manage. Admission to such a unit has to be arranged by the g.p.

geriatric day hospitals
Geriatric day hospitals are usually in hospital grounds, and patients attend one or more days a week for physiotherapy and occupational therapy. There is also general medical and nursing supervision. This maintenance treatment may enable an old person to remain at home who might otherwise need to be in hospital. Attendance at a day hospital can be arranged through the general practitioner and the geriatrician at the hospital.

transport
Anyone who can get to hospital either on public transport or in their own vehicle is expected to do so. Those who cannot will be collected by ambulance or hospital car service.

Where payment of the fare to get to and from hospital by public transport is a problem, the hospital social worker should be consulted: in certain circumstances, the fare may be fully or partially refunded.

health visitors
Health visitors are state registered nurses who have had additional training for their job. Although mainly working with mothers and

young children, health visitors also visit handicapped and elderly people; some are specifically geriatric health visitors. Their role is mainly advisory. They advise on all matters of health, also on other problems, practical and personal, and can suggest what facilities are available to meet the needs of the individual or household, such as nursing aids and equipment. A request for a visit should be made to the nearest health clinic or the general practitioner. Some g.p. practices have a health visitor working specifically with them.

In some areas, there is a preventative care clinic, often run by a health visitor under the supervision of a doctor, where elderly people can go for regular check-ups. These clinics, which have various names, such as keep well clinic or advisory health clinic, can be useful in identifying someone suffering from loss of mobility, sight or hearing or from foot problems, and referring the person for treatment.

home nursing
A nurse, usually nowadays called a district nursing sister, can be sent to patients by the general practitioner to undertake home nursing such as giving injections or a blanket bath. She is a qualified nurse who has taken additional training for her work in the community.

dentists
The general practitioner can usually arrange for a dentist to visit a patient at home, if essential; there is no extra charge to the patient.

Whether you have false teeth or your own, regular dental care is important. The difficulties of anyone whose speech is affected or who finds eating awkward are made worse by ill-fitting dentures.

prescription charges
As well as people over retirement age and those with incomes below a certain level, people with certain specified medical conditions requiring medication for long periods, or with a continuing physical disability, are exempt from paying national health service prescription charges. (Private patients must pay for all prescriptions.)

People who are not exempt and who need frequent prescriptions can get a pre-payment certificate, a kind of season ticket, for either six or twelve months (currently £2 and £3.50 respectively). This will cover all prescriptions during that period. Claim forms with further details can be obtained from any post office or social security office: form EC91 for exemption on the grounds of a medical condition, EC95 for a prepayment certificate.

Housing

Under the Chronically Sick and Disabled Persons Act 1970, housing authorities must give consideration to special accommodation for the disabled.

A few local authorities designate a proportion of all their new housing to disabled or elderly people: for instance, all the ground floor accommodation in a new housing estate may be allocated to them or purpose-built accommodation provided in the form of bungalows, flats or flatlets. Some authorities provide sheltered housing designed so that an elderly or disabled person can live independently and yet take advantage of communal facilities, with a warden available. Information about special housing locally can be obtained from the housing department or a housing advice centre. The social services department may also know of some private projects.

Voluntary organisations and housing associations put up purpose-built housing or adapt older houses for special needs. About a quarter of the member societies of the National Federation of Housing Societies provide housing entirely for the elderly. Some voluntary organisations helping particular disability groups, such as the British Rheumatism and Arthritis Association and the Multiple Sclerosis Society, have their own housing associations.

Young severely disabled people who have been brought up by relatives may need to go into sheltered accommodation either because this would give them more independence or because their relatives can no longer look after them. The variety of accommodation that may be available ranges from institutions providing total care to independent purpose-built flats with help on call. Hospital authorities provide young chronic sick units, and voluntary bodies, such as Habinteg Housing Association and John Grooms Housing Association, run various types of sheltered flats. The Cheshire Foundation runs both homes and sheltered accommodation consisting of flats and bungalows. The Central Council for the Disabled can give information about housing associations and other schemes of special housing for disabled people. Information about local schemes is obtainable from the local authority's social services and housing departments. There is a long waiting list for most places.

Residential homes
Going into a residential home, or even going to live with a relative, is a serious step and should not be taken just because other people are not prepared to face the risk that some accident may happen. It may be better to take all possible safety precautions in one's own home, including installing a telephone, if appropriate, and to arrange for all available services from the local authority, and assistance from voluntary organisations, in order to remain at home and independent as long as possible. However, it is only realistic to look forward to the time when residential accommodation may be needed. It is a wise move to visit possible places to gain a first-hand impression of the facilities and the inhabitants and to assess the suitability before applying to go on the waiting list. There are residential homes run by the local authority social services department, privately run ones, and homes run by voluntary organisations.

The social services departments have lists of the private homes registered in their area. The Elderly Invalids Fund gives information about voluntary and private residential homes and nursing homes in the Greater London area and can suggest sources for such information in other parts of the country. GRACE (Mrs. Gould's Residential Advisory Centre for the Elderly, Leigh Corner, Leigh Hill Road, Cobham, Surrey KT11 2HW) advises on private accommodation with or without nursing care in the southern half of England, not including Greater London, and maintains up to date information concerning vacancies.

Local authorities have the power to pay towards the cost of a disabled or elderly person living in private residential accommodation. When the whole cost of the fees has to be met by the individual or by relatives, the Supplementary Benefits Commission may grant an allowance towards the cost. For an elderly person, voluntary organisations such as the Distressed Gentlefolk's Aid Association (Vicarage Gate House, Vicarage Gate, London W8 4AQ) can sometimes help; the information service of the Elderly Invalids Fund (10 Fleet Street, London EC4Y 1BB) will give advice on and introductions to suitable benevolent funds.

If a disabled person who has been receiving a constant attendance allowance moves into accommodation for which the national health service or local authority pays, the allowance will be stopped after four weeks.

Information about aids

The Disabled Living Foundation (DLF) provides an information service for the disabled and an aids centre. Local authorities, hospitals, voluntary organisations, occupational therapists and many others subscribe to the information service, receive bi-monthly information sheets and are entitled to make enquiries on any problem concerning disabled people. Enquiries about specific problems, except those which are purely medical, may be made by disabled people themselves and their relatives. These will be answered free of charge, although donations are always welcome. Enquirers are asked to give as many details as are known about the problem so that as detailed information as possible can be supplied. The address of the Disabled Living Foundation is 346 Kensington High Street, London W14 8NS (telephone 01-602 2491). The Disabled Living Foundation's information service can give up to date information about manufacturers, stockists and prices of many of the aids mentioned in this book.

The DLF's aids centre at Kensington High Street, staffed by physiotherapists and occupational therapists, is a permanent display of a range of aids for disabled people. Some of these are aids specially designed for the disabled, others are ordinary household articles that experience has shown to be helpful. Aids are not on sale, but information on prices and sources of supply is available. The aids centre's main purpose is to provide practical information and a means of demonstration to doctors and other professional people, but disabled people and their relatives are welcome. It is necessary to make an appointment before visiting the centre in order to ensure that a therapist is available to show you round and explain the aids on display.

There is a Scottish Information Service for the Disabled (SISD) which operates in close liaison with the Disabled Living Foundation in London. The address is 18 Claremont Crescent, Edinburgh EH7 4QD (telephone 031-556 3882).

In some cities, aids centres are being set up in conjunction with the social services departments or local organisations for the disabled. For example, there is the Merseyside aids centre at Youens Way, East Prescot Road, Liverpool 14 (telephone 051-228 9221); the Newcastle upon Tyne aids centre at Mea House, Ellison Place, Newcastle upon Tyne NE1 8XS (telephone 0632-23617); the Birmingham Disabled Living Centre at 84 Suffolk Street, Birmingham 1 (telephone 021-643 0980). In Bristol, '0-90' is a business specializing in supplying aids where they can be tried out before buying.

The Central Council for the Disabled and the Spastics Society each send a travelling exhibition of aids around the country every year, where aids can be seen and handled and information obtained about suppliers and prices. The mobile centres stay a week or two in each place.

A series of booklets, *Equipment for the disabled*, each listing and illustrating selected equipment, was started by the National Fund for Research into Crippling Diseases (an organisation primarily concerned with raising funds for research projects). The series is compiled at Mary Marlborough Lodge and is now published by the Oxford regional health authority. The booklets are available (£1.50 each, plus postage) from 2 Foredown Drive, Portslade, Sussex BN4 2BB.

The NFRCD also sponsored the Research Institute for Consumer Affairs' comparative tests for the disabled user, and the RICA reports (40p) are available from the NFRCD, Vincent House, 1 Springfield Road, Horsham, Sussex RH12 2BR.

The illustrated catalogues of mail order suppliers of aids can be useful in showing what is available.

Certain aids considered essential for the disabled are specifically zero-rated for value added tax. Also, an aid required to relieve a severe abnormality or injury and authorised by a doctor can be zero-rated. This includes wheelchairs, adjustable beds, commode chairs, chair lifts, hoists, adapted or special cutlery.

There is much that can be done around the home to make life more comfortable and more pleasant for someone who has become disabled and to eliminate possible hazards. Even minor modifications can go a long way towards this. Major modifications are worth considering to adapt a house to accommodate someone who is heavily handicapped for whom the alternative would have to be residential care.

Designing for the disabled by Selwyn Goldsmith, published by the Royal Institute of British Architects, offers architectural design criteria in relation to people with physical disabilities. *Safety in the home,* design bulletin 13, produced by the Department of the Environment and available from Her Majesty's Stationery Offices, shows how to take safety into account when designing a home, and includes useful information on floor coverings.

Floor coverings
A disabled or elderly person is more liable to accidents in the home than a younger, more ablebodied person, and the possible consequences of a fall are likely to be more disabling. Therefore, it is important to reduce the risks of falling as much as possible.

All floor and stair coverings should be in good condition: torn lino and threadbare carpets are hazardous. Fitted carpets are good because they produce an uninterrupted non-slippery surface. But a carpet with too thick a pile can be immobilising for someone who shuffles, and will create resistance for a wheelchair user.

Someone who is determined to keep loose rugs and mats should put non-slip underlay between floor and rug, or tack down the rug or mat, so that the edges cannot be kicked up. Rather than using a mat to try to cut down the draught from an ill-fitting door, some form of draught excluder should be fixed to the door instead.

An uncarpeted floor should ideally not be polished at all; if you must, use a non-slip polish.

Stairs
A stair carpet should be firmly fixed down. Where there are worn patches, the stair carpet should be moved so that the worn part comes on the riser not the tread.

Old worn wooden stairs can be levelled by filling the worn area with a liquid compound which sets hard and level. To do this, the front of the tread is built up to its original height by nailing a strip of wood along it, and the floor-fill paste is poured into the hollow behind the strip. This paste sets within an hour and can be walked on the same day.

To show where steps are or stairs begin, a strip of shiny white tape can be stuck along the edge of the top and bottom step.

A second banister rail gives additional support on a narrow staircase and, for someone with only one useful hand, may be needed to provide a rail both for going upstairs and for coming downstairs. The rail should extend beyond the stairs at both top and bottom by about 18 inches (about 460 mm) in order to give support when stepping off the top and bottom steps because the hand on the rail should always be a step ahead of the feet. (If this is impracticable because a corridor is at right angles to the staircase, you can still get support from the rail if you turn towards the end of the rail.) Similar rails may also be needed alongside any odd steps—for instance, halfway along a corridor or down to a kitchen or lavatory.

Someone with a heart or chest condition may find it less tiring to go upstairs backwards. People with stiff hips may prefer to go up backwards because less hip bend is needed, or may go up sideways with the back sliding up the wall. Some people can only go up by putting the stronger or more mobile leg up first, and bringing the other to join it. Coming down, the weaker leg goes first.

Going downstairs backwards may be better for someone who lacks confidence. You cannot see the drop of stairs ahead and do not have to project the weight forward on to the step below. Reach down backwards with one leg, and tuck the toes well into the angle of the stairs before transferring weight on to the foot. To negotiate stairs backwards, you need to have a handrail all the way.

Another solution, especially with high steps, is to use half-steps, which reduce each step to half its height along a third of its length.

They entail climbing twice the number of steps but each one will be easier. Wooden half-steps, made by a carpenter or competent handyman, need to be screwed firmly to each stair. It may not be possible to put half-steps on spiral stairs or on a staircase with narrow winders. Outdoor concrete steps can be built up into half-steps with cement.

A portable half-step can be made by fixing a piece of wood on to the end of a long walking stick. The walking stick must be longer than usual so that the person using it can reach down and pick it up from the step below. A hollow half-step minimises the weight. A portable half-step can be difficult to use: it is not very stable and may not fit on to awkward corners on the stairs. But it may be worth trying as a temporary measure or for use in other people's houses.

The Step-stick is a walking stick with a folding metal piece that comes down at the touch of a toe to form a stepping ledge $4\frac{1}{2}$ inches (about 110 mm) high. It can be used indoors on stairs or out of doors—for instance, to get on to a bus.

Someone who is unable to walk up and down stairs may manage to sit up them instead. If the stairs are too steep for this method, a half-step with one sloping side may be the answer. Sitting on one side of the stair, slide up the wedge and on to the portable step, and then push up on to the stair above. Pick up the half-step and place it ready for use on the opposite side of the stairs. If this method works well, it may be worth fixing a series of wedge half-steps up the staircase on alternate sides of the stairs.

lifts
Instead of undertaking major structural alterations to a house in order to enable someone who cannot manage stairs to live downstairs, installing some kind of a lift may be more practical, and in some cases more economical.

—stair lifts
A stair lift is a platform which travels up and down a staircase on tracks either on the stairs themselves or on the adjoining wall. This latter arrangement is neater and leaves more of the stairs clear.

Some models of stair lift have a fixed seat and others have a folding seat so that the user can either sit or stand. Others consist of a platform to stand on with a rail to hold on to. With most models, the seat and the platform fold back against the wall when not in use. Some stair lifts are designed to take a wheelchair.

Most stair lifts are designed to go up a straight staircase. Where there is a landing at the top of one flight of stairs and then a further flight of no more than three additional steps, it may be possible, provided there is sufficient room, to extend the stair lift above the top step of the first flight and then build a platform across to the top of the next level. If a staircase is made up of two long flights with a landing between, it would be necessary to install two stair lifts, and cross the landing from one to the other. But this almost doubles the cost. There are stair lifts which have specially curved rails to negotiate bends, but these cost twice as much as a straight stair lift.

The installation costs for a stair lift are usually much lower than for a vertical lift because there is little building work involved, no making holes in the ceiling, replastering and redecorating. The only problem may be finding somewhere to house the electric driving unit which can be quite large. A stair lift also has the advantage that it can be dismantled if the user moves house.

—vertical lifts
There are basically two different types of vertical lift: those which are encased in a shaft and those which run on guide rails or wall tracks and are not enclosed. A lift inside a shaft is not necessarily more expensive

than one on wall tracks. The smallest lift takes one person standing up.

There are different types of lift compartments. A lift within a shaft has a completely enclosed compartment with a door. A lift which runs on guide rails may have an enclosed compartment or may simply be a platform with rails round it. An open type of compartment has the advantage of eliminating the need for opening and closing lift doors; but safety rails must be secured.

The wall track type of lift usually takes up less apparent space than a lift shaft. As it rises to the floor above, it either emerges into a box built over the hole, or raises a trap door which falls back into place when the lift goes down, leaving maximum floor area in the room above. Coming down, there is a magic eye which stops the lift if anyone or anything is underneath it.

It is sometimes possible in a big house to fit a lift into the stair well. Otherwise, a hole has to be cut in the ceiling and floor of the level above. Besides finding suitable space for the lift, it will be necessary to have somewhere to house the mechanism. Lift manufacturers will send representatives to visit and advise on these problems.

Lighting and switches

Adequate and convenient lighting on stairs and along corridors is essential. It may be necessary to put in better positioned switches or two-way switches in order to be able to switch off a light without having to go back.

There should be lights in all at-risks areas, not only in obvious places such as the top, bottom and turns of staircases, but also in the larder, the cupboard under the stairs, the coalshed, the front porch, the garage, an outside lavatory and the path down to it.

With increasing age, you may need stronger light both for reading and everyday tasks. This may simply mean re-positioning a light or putting more powerful bulbs into existing lights (the extra electricity used is negligible). It may mean changing lampshades. Some shades direct the light more suitably than others for reading or sewing. On some shades it is specified that the shade must not be used with a powerful light bulb because it would melt or scorch.

Rocker action light switches are easier to operate than the old-fashioned dolly switches. When a dolly switch is difficult to reach, a screw eye at the end of a wooden stick can be useful to hook it up and down.

A footpress switch could be installed at floor level for someone who finds it difficult to operate a switch by hand. There is also a switch which works from the warmth of any part of the body held against it, such as the hand or chin. On a table lamp and other electrical appliances you could have a low pressure air switch installed, which can be operated by very light manual pressure or can be fitted with a mouthpiece and operated by blowing.

By connecting a lamp to a time switch, it can be set to come on automatically at any time required. There are also light-sensitive devices which switch on when it gets dark.

Trailing flexes are a hazard. Where there is an adequate number of socket outlets, positioned where they are most needed, the flex between each appliance and its power source can be short. If the appliance has to be some way from the socket outlet, the flex should be long enough to be hooked along the skirting board so that it does not trail. Flex should never be covered by a carpet or rug.

Socket outlets can be fixed at any height to suit the users. The *Which?* report on electric socket heights (September 1971) found that for both the ablebodied and the handicapped, the best compromise height was 39 inches (about 1 metre) above the floor.

A plug with a handle to make it easier to grasp is made by Rentoul Workshops (Truro, Cornwall). For general safety, it is better to have a switched socket than to have to take a plug in and out frequently to disconnect an appliance.

Remote control switches are designed to enable you to switch an electrical appliance on or off without having to go to the appliance. Someone sitting in a chair can control, for example, lights, a radio, an electric blanket. To fix up remote control switches is a one-off job that should be done by a competent electrician. Not every appliance can be so controlled; there would be difficulty with a heater, a cooker or other high powered appliance which would require a heavier flex or special switching.

A remote control switch can be fitted to switch any television set on and off, provided it has been pre-set to the correct channel. There are expensive remote controlled colour television sets, on which channels, brightness, colour and volume can be changed from a distance.

Heating

Someone who is unable to move around easily is likely to feel the cold more. Some form of central heating is the ideal way of providing constant warmth. In a home without central heating, electric night storage heaters may be a good way of providing this. A disabled person, particularly someone in a wheelchair, is more likely to need to have doors left open, and therefore background heating in every room is desirable, preferably thermostatically controlled to maintain the right temperature. A less mobile person often needs more heat than the rest of the family so supplementary heating may be necessary in particular parts of the house.

Help yourself to warmth, an action broadsheet for health, social and voluntary workers, available from Age Concern, suggests ways of getting money to help with heating costs and of getting more heat for your money.

Heating costs a lot of money. Efficiency will be higher and running costs reduced with good insulation. Lagging in the loft, double glazing, draught-excluding strips on doors and windows, can all help.

If you have an open solid fuel fire, it is probably better to keep a large container near the fire, for the coal, which can be replenished in small quantities that are easier to carry. Keeping a stool or chair near the fire enables you to sit down to tend the fire without stooping over it. There are slow-burning stoves that function with the doors open and require minimal upkeep. With the doors closed, the fire will stay in for some hours or even overnight. But the ashes have to be emptied while they are still hot, and this is hazardous. It is best to empty the ashcan frequently so that it does not get too heavy.

Any open or radiant fire should have a separate guard, at least 8 inches (about 200 mm) in front of the fire for safety. Do not keep ornaments that need frequent dusting or a clock that needs winding or a mirror on the mantelpiece above an open fire.

Although paraffin stoves are cheap and provide a lot of warmth, they are on the whole not a suitable form of heating for an elderly person nor for most disabled people. New paraffin stoves are designed so that they extinguish themselves if they are knocked over, but an old paraffin stove may be a hazard. All oil stoves have to be filled frequently, with the risk that someone who is at all shaky will spill paraffin. A paraffin stove must never be carried while it is alight.

Gas fires can be efficient room heaters, especially the type that combines convection with radiation. When buying a gas heater, choose one with controls that you can manipulate easily. A large single rotary lever control provides the best grip. Some gas fires have the controls at the top, some are lit by simply turning a knob. A gas fire with a thermostat to maintain the temperature eliminates the need for manual adjustment of the heat control from time to time.

Electric fires, if not built in, can raise problems of plugs and flexes. If the socket outlet is conveniently positioned, an electric heater can be more versatile than a gas one. For instance, you can have the switch where you can reach it from bed so that you do not need to get up until the room is warm. But small lightweight electric radiant fires are a potential hazard because they can be easily tipped over. Wall-mounted heaters are safest. The heater should not be placed too high up on the wall because it may not then keep your legs and feet warm enough. A time switch can be used with any electric fire to turn it on or off at set times.

Each area electricity board has home economists or other trained staff who can be asked for help or advice about the use of electrical equipment or adaptations. The home service division of the local gas region can be asked for advice on the use of gas appliances by a disabled person. A free safety check of gas appliances used by a handicapped person can be arranged by the gas region if the person's name is submitted by a social worker from the local authority or an organisation for the disabled.

A free booklet, *Danger from fire,* prepared for the Home Office by the Central Office of Information, gives hints on how to protect your home from fire hazards. It is available from local fire brigades and direct from the Home Office (Horseferry House, Dean Ryle Street, London SW1P 2AW).

gas and electricity meters

Slot meters are often in places difficult to reach, tucked away at the back of a low cupboard or high up on the wall. The gas and electricity authorities can be asked to move their meters to a more accessible position. (The charge for doing this is in some cases waived or met by the local social services department.)

Putting the money into the meter can be a problem. A handle with a longer lever arm to make the operation of a gas meter easier can be bought from the gas board. With a gas slot meter, when the money runs out, the pilot light on an appliance gives out, and there is a danger that a gas tap may have been left on.

It may be better to change to quarterly payment, putting money aside regularly towards the expected bill. Special stamps (for example, for 50p) can be bought at gas and electricity showrooms to use to pay a quarterly account when it comes. Most gas and electricity authorities have budget account systems so that payment can be made monthly, calculated on the assessment of annual consumption, adjusted as necessary at the end of the year.

Windows

It is easier to open a window if it is possible to get close up to it, so a large piece of furniture such as a table should not be placed underneath a window. Someone who is disabled or elderly should never stand on a chair to open or close a window.

Windows open more easily if they are in good repair. The hinges and fastenings of casement windows should be paint free, and oiled regularly so that they move freely. Handles can be enlarged to make them easier to grip.

The top part of a sash window can usually be more easily opened if a ring is screwed into the middle of the top and a long pole with a hook on the end is used to move it up and down. To open the lower half, a pulley system could be used.

Pivoted windows are probably the easiest for a disabled person to manage: they pivot horizontally from central points at each side and the only effort required is pulling a cord. Remote control winding gear can be fitted for a fanlight window or any other window that is out of reach—for someone in a wheelchair, for instance.

A cord-operated curtain control that works on a pulley system makes it easier to open and close curtains. Blinds and curtains can be opened and closed electrically by remote control by fitting a small motor to operate the pull-cord type of curtain runner.

Venetian blinds can be used to give privacy, especially in a ground floor room, without obstructing much light or interfering with the outward view. They may be easier to handle than curtains but are laborious to clean.

Doors
It is easier to get through a door that opens towards you if you can approach it obliquely from the handle side rather than from the hinge side. This avoids the need to move the feet or the wheelchair to get out of the way of the door as it opens. Someone in a wheelchair may find it helpful to have a horizontal rail put on the door so that he can reach back and close it behind him. Doors can be fitted with a sash weight which reduces the effort to open and close them. Where there is a double door, it will be more easily opened if it is fitted with extra long bolts, top and bottom, to bring them within reach. A spring-loaded bolt with a chain attached can be operated from a wheelchair.

Where it is awkward to open a door, it may be feasible to rehang the door to open the other way, or a sliding door or a folding door could be substituted. In some situations, a door can be taken away. A curtain of plastic strips could be put up instead of a door; this is easy to get through. A sliding door takes up no room space when it is opened but needs wall space.

From a wheelchair, a sliding door with both top and bottom runners is easiest to operate: if the door is held on top runners only, it will tend to twist because someone in a wheelchair has to grasp the door low down. The channel for the bottom runners must be set into the floor so as not to form an obstacle.

Some doorways have a raised threshold, which can be a hazard. This should, if possible, be removed or levelled with a ramp.

—door handles and keys
A roller catch allows a door to be opened and closed by pressure against it, without having to manipulate a door handle.,

A lever handle is easier to operate than a knob provided it is working freely; sometimes the final push needs too much force. Where the knob is an integral part of the lock and therefore cannot be easily changed to a lever handle, an adjustable leather strip attached to a wooden handle can be used to help turn the knob.

The lock on a door may need to be repositioned to come within the reach of someone in a wheelchair.

Turning a key can be difficult for someone whose grip is weak. The lock must be kept lubricated—with graphite, not oil which would become clogged with dirt. There are several ways of increasing your leverage on a key. The simplest is to put a piece of dowelling or a skewer through the hole in the key head. Alternatively, a yale type of key can be fitted on to a piece of wood and secured with a screw through the hole in the key.

—*front door*

Anyone who is old or disabled is right to be cautious about opening the door to strangers. A one-way peephole which enables the person inside to see out but not the person outside to see in is a useful precaution on the front door. It is also sometimes possible to fix a mirror outside the window of a room at such an angle that you can see who the caller is before you go to the door. A chain across the door is an additional safeguard.

Someone who is immobile or very slow at getting to the front door would benefit from the remote control and intercom system used in some blocks of flats: the caller rings the bell, the occupant asks through the intercom who it is and, if the caller is acceptable, presses a button to allow the front door to open.

Letter flaps in front doors often have no container to catch the letters put through. If you find it difficult to pick letters up from the floor, fit a wire container to catch the letters (provided this does not prevent the door from opening fully enough to allow a wheelchair through). Wire makes it possible to see from a distance whether there are any letters without having to go all the way to the front door.

—electrically operated doors

Electrically operated doors are available but are extremely expensive and need special wiring and fitting. The electrical mechanism can be worked by pulling a cord, pressing a button, by elbow contact or stepping on a contact mat. Doors can also be operated by a photocell light beam. The disadvantage is that the mechanism can be triggered off by anyone who walks by.

—garage doors

It may be worth considering an electrically operated door for the garage to save having to get out of a car to open the garage door. There are several electrically operated garage doors on the market, and it is also possible to convert some up-and-over doors to operate electrically.

Of the manually operated garage doors, an up-and-over door requires little strength but considerable reach. This may be a problem for someone in a wheelchair, but fixing a rope to the top and bottom edges of the door may enable it to be pulled open or shut, in a similar way to a centrally pivoting window. Bolts on sliding or hinged doors may be hard to manipulate or out of reach. Spring loaded top and bottom bolts could be fitted, connected by a chain or wire so that they can be freed by a pull at any level.

B

Intercom systems

An intercom system is useful for keeping in touch with other people in the household if you are isolated for part of the day because of living in another part of the house—upstairs, for example, or in an extension. It can also be used to link someone with a neighbour in a nearby house, provided the intercom system has sufficient range.

Mains-operated systems of the type used in offices which must be specially wired in are expensive to install.

There are many battery-operated two-way systems of the baby alarm type. These come supplied with a connecting lead varying in length from 50 to 650 feet (about 15 to 190 metres). Most of these systems are controlled from one end, and only one person can talk at a time. The set is switched either to talk or listen. It can be left switched on so that you can call into it for attention at any time; with some, it is necessary to bleep your end to attract the attention of the person at the other end, who then switches on the system.

Telephone

If you live alone, or spend a large part of the day alone, it is important to be able to get help readily in case of an accident or illness, or an inability to manage. The best system for most people is to have a telephone. This not only provides a means of communicating with the doctor or a social worker, but is also a way of keeping in touch with relatives and friends. Grown-up children may find it difficult to visit often but, with a telephone they can check up regularly every day to make sure all is well and unanswered calls will act as an alarm signal.

Local authorities are empowered to provide telephones for those in need, under the terms of the Chronically Sick and Disabled Persons Act. Need is not defined in the Act but local authorities have drawn up minimum criteria. Either the medical or non-medical criteria have to be met in full and apply only if no family, friends or neighbours are available and willing and able to help. The medical criteria are that a person has a prima facie need to get in touch with the doctor quickly and is in danger when left alone unless provided with a telephone, and lives alone or, if not, is regularly and frequently left alone. The non-medical criteria are that the person lives alone, has at least one person with whom to be in touch by telephone, is unable in normal weather to leave the house without the help of another person, and, in the view of the local authority, needs a telephone to avoid isolation.

These criteria are issued for guidance to local authorities; they are not in themselves binding and are open to different interpretations. In any particular situation, the local authority considers whether a problem is best solved by providing a telephone or by some other means. In the case of a husband and wife living together, the local authority will consider the medical condition of both and the extent to which the least handicapped partner is able to maintain contact with their doctor without a telephone.

Some authorities are more generous than others. Someone who needs a telephone but who seems outside the recommended criteria should not hesitate to ask to be considered. However, someone who has always had a telephone and can well afford to continue paying for it should not expect to be subsidised because of becoming disabled.

Anyone who is hoping to have a telephone installed by the local authority should check first on what is meant by providing a telephone. Some local authorities pay the installation fee; some pay the rental but not the cost of any calls; some meet the cost for the first year but not after that.

A telephone is of little use in an emergency to someone who is frightened of the instrument and has difficulty in using it. You should therefore ask for help with learning to use it, and practise making calls.

The Post Office issue a leaflet, *Help for the handicapped*, describing ways of helping a handicapped or disabled person who has problems using a telephone. The equipment they can offer includes a transistorised amplifier in the earpiece, an additional earpiece to reduce interference from other noises, a faint-speech amplifier for someone with a permanently weak voice, a device which connects the caller direct to the operator by pressing on a button and is useful for someone who cannot use a telephone dial, call-makers programmed to dial calls automatically at the press of a button or by inserting a card, hand-free telephones with an inbuilt loudspeaker and microphone, and a lightweight headset which also eliminates the need to hold the handset to the ear. The Post Office will also supply a switchboard operator's dialling aid which fits on to the end of a pencil to make a dialling stick to dial with instead of an outstretched finger. Push button systems which are easier to operate than normal dials are now available in some areas. The local telephone sales office can be asked what special arrangements can be offered to meet particular needs.

Apart from Post Office appliances, there are other telephone aids that leave the hands free when telephoning, such as a special amplifier or devices to hold the handset above the desk at shoulder height or on the shoulder (someone with sloping shoulders may have difficulty in keeping it from slipping off). With one type of telephone aid, the handset is left permanently in the up-ended position and a bar or lever is placed on the telephone rest for connection and disconnection. Post Office engineers advise against this because the carbon grains in the handset need to be shaken up to work effectively, as happens automatically in normal use.

Emergency call systems
Probably the best alarm system is to have a good neighbour. Someone who is regularly in contact will be able to help with all kinds of minor problems and alert the doctor or a social worker if necessary.

There is a variety of emergency call systems available. Research undertaken by the Institute for Consumer Ergonomics in 1974 to evaluate the various systems showed that none of them was ideal. Some did not work in an emergency and therefore could give a false sense of security.

When choosing an alarm system, the first point to decide is its purpose—for emergency use in the case of a sudden illness or accident or mainly for the reassurance of being in touch with someone—and who will be called by the alarm. Too many systems are installed without making sure that someone is going to answer the alarm when it is set off.

An alarm must be reliable. Many portable alarms are powered by batteries that have a relatively short life. With many alarm systems, particularly those which operate flashing lights at a distance, there is no way the user can tell if the alarm is working.

The simplest form of alarm system is to put a card in the window to attract the attention of a passer-by. It is also possible to buy a flashing light unit to put in the window which, when switched on, illuminates a sign showing an address to be contacted. Some also have a buzzer which rings outside to draw attention to the flashing light. These systems do not work unless someone has been alerted to watch out for the sign appearing in the window. The drawback inherent in a scheme that puts out a general alarm call rather than alerting a specific person is that the alarm may be an open invitation to an intruder to come into the house where someone is helpless.

There are alarms such as hand-held buzzers, sirens or whistles which are useless unless carried around all the time. The alarm must therefore be lightweight, small and relatively unobtrusive so that it is not a nuisance to carry, and must also be robust because it is likely to get knocked and probably dropped from time to time. Alarms in the form of a buzzer or siren are operated by a switch, a press button or a pull-out pin. Most have a rather low noise output and would probably not be heard from outside the house or through an intervening wall.

Remote control alarms, operated by a transmitter, also must be carried around all the time. These alarms activate a strategically placed bell or flashing light or hooter or buzzer. They are only appropriate if the alarm can be fixed where someone can be relied on to take action if it goes off. A light which flashes inside a neighbour's house or a buzzer which sounds under her window, for instance, can act as an effective alarm. The transmitter must be easy to get at and operate, but should not easily go off inadvertently. The range of signal even within the house is reduced by obstacles such as walls, baths or metal radiators. Radio transmitters need to be licensed. A licence has to be applied for on form BR 12 from the Radio Regulatory Division of the Home Office and costs £4.80 for a year. If your local authority provides transmitter alarms, it may have a bulk licence that covers all the transmitters it supplies.

There are alarms operated by switches, buttons or pull cords at fixed positions. With some systems, a number of controlling points can be provided so that there is one in each room. But someone who has fallen may not be able to get to a switch. With overhead pull switches it may be wise to have them in a distinctive colour so that they do not get confused with pull switches for lights. Fixed switch systems activate an alarm at a fixed point, for example in a neighbour's house. The alarm takes the form of a flashing light or a siren or a hooter.

There are temperature control systems activated automatically when the temperature rises above a certain point, as in a fire, or falls below a certain point, when the house is becoming unhealthily cold.

Habit cycle alarms work on the principle that if the system is not regularly reset by a normal daily activity, such as flushing the lavatory or treading on a mat, an alarm automatically goes off. Automatic alarms can also be linked to the conscious action of operating a reset switch at specified intervals: if the switch is not reset, a buzzer sounds on the alarm control and if the switch is then not reset, an external alarm is set off. This type of system is the only one that comes into action even if the person is unable to do anything at all to switch it on. But someone who is immobilised by an accident may have to wait up to 12 or even 24 hours for help.

For someone who spends more than the average time sitting down, the choice of a suitable chair is important.

Easy chairs

A chair should be comfortable and give the right support. It should be stable, durable and strong, because you may put the whole weight of your body on one side of it when rising, or may fall back heavily with a bump on sitting down. The RICA comparative test report No 6 (July 1970) deals with easy chairs for the elderly.

Any chair should allow for changes in position because this reduces the discomfort of sitting in one position all the time and relieves pressure on the parts of the body pressing on the chair. Someone who has to remain sitting for long periods should learn to relieve sitting pressure periodically in order to avoid pressure sores. Those with spinal cord injury who have no sensation are taught to do this as a habit.

When trying out a chair before buying one, check not only that it is comfortable when sitting in a variety of positions—upright or more slumped or more sideways—but that you can get up from it easily.

The height of the seat is important. Getting up from a low seat is much more difficult than rising from a high seat, which is why many so-called geriatric chairs are specially high, usually 18 inches (about 460 mm) or more. Ideally, when sitting, the hips, knees and ankles should be at right angles, and you should be able to move the feet easily to different positions with the heel on the floor. Foot and ankle movement is especially important if you have cold or swollen feet because it helps to promote the circulation; otherwise there may be difficulty in getting up and walking. This height seat also means that weight is taken by the buttocks, not the soft tissue behind the knee where pressure would not only be uncomfortable but interfere with the circulation.

A few manufacturers offer a choice of height for some of their chairs. It is also possible to buy chairs with legs that are adjustable in height in the same way as metal crutches; these make the chair look rather clinical.

A favourite chair that is too low can probably be raised by a competent handyman. Most types of chair leg can be lengthened with angle iron screwed to the chair legs and plastic pieces fitted over the metal ends or by using wooden blocks.

Chairs can be made higher by replacing an existing cushion with a firmer one, or placing an additional cushion on top. To prevent the top cushion slipping, a piece of non-slip carpet underlay can be inserted between the two. But raising the height of the chair in this way can make the arms too low.

—seats

A chair seat needs to be short enough from front to back to allow for sitting with the back well supported and the feet firmly on the floor. Ideally, there should be a space of two or three inches between the front of the chair seat and the back of the knees so that there is no pressure against the back of the knees. If the chair seat is too long, the person sitting in it will be forced to slump backwards into the chair in order to rest the shoulders against the back and also to avoid uncomfortable pressure behind the knees.

If the chair seat is too soft and yielding, it may not give sufficient support and also will increase the difficulties of rising. If it is too hard (and you sit down too rapidly), it can be uncomfortable. A firm base with a soft resilient surface is probably best. A chair without arms should have a firm front edge to make pushing up into the standing position easier.

A seat covering made from a smooth, slightly slippery material makes movement easier, in particular sliding to the front of the seat in preparation for getting up from the chair. PVC and similarly coated materials would be suitable, but may become hot and uncomfortable, because they do not absorb moisture.

A chair seat which slopes down towards the back of the chair is generally more comfortable, and helps to prevent someone who falls asleep from sliding forward in the chair. But if getting out of the chair is difficult, a firmly stuffed wedge-shaped cushion can be used to level the seat. Such a cushion can also be used to convert an ordinary seat to slope backwards in order to prevent the occupant sliding out. It is possible to buy a harness to prevent someone falling or sliding down in a chair, but this must be in the right place: attached to the top of the back chair legs and the strap fastened across the hip bones.

In time, the supporting webbing of a chair seat begins to sag, the cushions lose their resilience and the chair begins to well in the middle. This welling is not always visually apparent. To check someone's chair, take a turn of sitting in it for an hour or so to judge whether the seat frame can be felt through the seat cushioning and is causing pressure under the thighs. If the chair springs have sagged, a piece of stout plywood placed over them resting on the frame under the cushion will prevent sinking too low into the chair.

—backs

The ideal height for the chair back depends on the purpose for which a chair is being used. An easy chair is more comfortable if it provides support for the head and shoulders; a working chair can have a much shorter back but should come to above the bottom of the shoulder blades.

When someone nods off to sleep in a chair, the head usually falls forward until the chin almost reaches the chest, and then tends to loll sideways, with the body inclining in the same direction. A chair with wings would give some support in this position. Some chairs have a high back with a head rest and others come with a neck cushion. A

japanese neck pillow can be comfortable; attached to a strip of material with a weight at the end, it can be left in position over the back of the chair, like an antimacassar. You can make a neck pillow from a small soft pillow tied tightly round the middle.

A well designed chair back should give good support in the lumbar region. Some chairs are made with a specially moulded bulge to fit into the lumbar curve. This can be very comfortable provided the contour of your back fits the contour of the chair. But the bulge may come in just the wrong place, so it is particularly important to try out this type of chair before buying one. An extra cushion in the lumbar region may be more comfortable. It is possible to buy a specially shaped cushion designed to give lumbar support.

Some chairs have a back which can be adjusted to different positions so that it can be fixed at the angle you find most comfortable.

—arms

The arms of the chair need to be low enough to let your arms rest comfortably without humping the shoulders, but should not interfere with movement—for example, when knitting.

Arm rests need to be high enough to be useful when rising from the chair. There comes a point when having pushed up so far towards standing, it is necessary to release the grip on the arm rests and straighten up without their help. This is easier with arm rests that project well forward. When the arms project beyond the front of the seat, the front legs of the chair should slope forward so that there is no danger of tipping the chair when pressing down on the arms. One advantage of a higher chair is that the arm rests are high in relation to the floor and therefore give extra support. With a lower chair, arm rests which slope upwards towards the front of the chair will help.

If you have to support yourself on an elbow or forearm rather than just the hands when getting up from a chair, you will need high arm rests, even though these may be in the way when knitting or sewing.

Padded arm rests are more comfortable but less easy to grasp. Those with padded arms and bare wooden ends are probably best.

Filled-in sides to the chair help to keep out draughts and make it easier to keep a handbag and papers beside you. Or you can fasten a bag to the arm of the chair so that you have books, your spectacles, knitting and newspaper to hand, without having to keep asking someone to fetch things for you.

getting up from a chair

A basic method of standing up from a chair is as follows:

1. Lean forward, bringing the head and shoulders over the knees.
2. Move forward on the seat. There are various alternative methods: to pull on the chair arms and slide forward; or wriggle forward by

transferring weight to one hip, then pushing the other hip forward, and then repeating the movement; or push up on the chair arms to raise the hips from the seat, lowering them farther forward, and repeating as necessary.

3. Place the feet firmly on the floor, and slightly apart. One foot should be slightly in front of the knee and the other slightly behind and under the edge of the seat: this helps to bring the body weight over the feet and you will be in a stable position when you are standing (but it cannot be done if there is a low cross rail between the front legs of the chair). Alternatively, draw both feet back under the body, keeping them wide apart: this means that you get a better thrust to stand up but will be in a less stable position once standing.

4. Lean forward, with the hands on the front of the chair arms.

5. Press down on the chair arms to raise the hips.

6. Still leaning forward, transfer the weight forward by straightening your arms and to a lesser extent the knees.

7. Fully straighten the hips and knees to stand erect with the weight over the feet, raising your head at the same time to look straight ahead.

The last movement may be difficult because you have to let go of the arm rests while still some way from the upright position. A walking aid placed two or three inches in front of the chair or a solid piece of furniture nearby that can be grasped may give the necessary confidence.

You should learn to go through these motions as a continuous action because the momentum will help you to rise. It sometimes helps to count 'one, two, three' and start rising at 'three'.

There are various ways of helping someone up from a chair. At all stages, the helper should be in a position of balance ready to give support. It is usually safer for the helper to stand beside the chair, on the person's weaker side, with one foot pointing forward in the direction of movement and the rear foot towards the chair. From this position, it is easy to take a step forward to support the person as he rises. It is better to give support under the elbow than under the armpit, and to support rather than lift or pull.

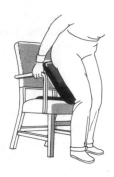

—self-lift seats

A spring-assisted lifting seat is designed to lift the seat from the horizontal to an angle of 45°. There are two parts to such a seat; the top part is hinged at the front and is held up by a strong spring. As the person sits down, the seat folds beneath him; when he begins to rise, the spring helps him up. These seats are not very satisfactory on a fully upholstered chair, only on one with a very firm base.

Someone with generalised weakness or painful joints may find a self-lift seat of benefit. These seats are not usually recommended for anyone with poor balance, and are not designed to help anyone with really stiff hips or knees.

Self-lift seats only begin to work when the person has started to rise by leaning forward and taking some weight on his feet. The rising mechanism is not strong enough to lift the whole body weight. The person is pushed forward to the three-quarter standing position but must be able to get himself up from there. This final part of rising, where the arm supports have been left behind, is difficult and therefore these seats are of limited use.

More elaborate are chairs incorporating a self-lift seat. These have springs which are mechanically or electrically operated and this mechanism must be gauged correctly for the weight of the user. Wrongly weighted, it may be either ineffective or dangerous.

There is an electrically operated lifting chair (the Motor Riser) in which the chair arms rise with the seat and contact is maintained with the seat and arms as the sitter is slowly raised to a standing position.

sitting down in a chair
1. Get near enough to feel the front of the chair with the back of both legs.
2. Keeping your weight over the feet, bend your knees and hips and let your hands rest on the arms of the chair.
3. Gradually shift your weight backwards from the feet, supporting yourself on your hands as you sit down.
4. Move back in the chair, in the reverse action from getting up, until the base of your spine is against the chair back.

Someone who has to fall into a chair because of weak or uncoordinated legs or stiff knees needs not only a strong chair but one with backward extending legs. Sitting down may be easier to manage by leaning one arm on the arm rest and swivelling round into the chair.

When sitting down in a chair without arms, bend the knees and hips until the heel of the hand rests on the edge of the seat (do not try to take the weight on the fingers, either with the palm outstretched or with the hand in a fist).

special chairs
A rocking chair which rocks gently through only a small range of movement and has a firm base provides gentle exercise for the legs.

It is sometimes useful to have a chair in which a person can be wheeled about. A metal frame with wheels can be bought to fit under any size of chair to convert it to a wheeled chair. But this increases the height of the seat by several inches. There are also special chairs with either two or four castors. Many of these have safety devices so that the wheels will turn only when the chair is pushed, not when the occupant moves involuntarily. But although it may seem a good idea to be able to get quickly from, say, the fireside to the dining table, it may be better to be encouraged to walk. A doctor or therapist should be consulted beforehand about the usefulness of such equipment for you.

—for those with stiff hips
Someone with fairly stiff hips needs an armchair with a very sloping back. For sitting up at a desk or table, if you can bend the knee sufficiently, it may be possible to use an upright chair by sitting on the

front of the seat and tucking the leg under the chair. The seat of the chair should be reasonably soft and there must be no cross bar to get in the way.

An office type of chair can have a section of one side of the seat cut out to make it suitable for someone with one stiff hip.

For someone with two stiff hips, there are stools, adjustable in height, with motor cycle saddle seats and some with a back rest. These make good working seats.

An alternative is a kitchen stool with about two inches cut off the front legs. This alters the stress on the joints of the stool and the stool must therefore be a strong one; a flimsy stool would soon collapse. Non-slip rubber tips should be put on the legs of the stool, if possible, to give it extra stability.

—reclining-platform chairs
A severely disabled person with very stiff hips and knees or a stiff spine may be unable to fit into any chair or stool, let alone get up again. The Powell Seat Company makes special chairs which are really reclining platforms. These allow the person to move from an almost horizontal 'sitting' position to an upright position by turning a handle. Such a chair takes up a lot of space in a room but can give a considerable measure of independence to someone who has previously been immobilised.

The standing aid made by Godfrey Engineering enables someone with paralysed legs to raise himself from a sitting to a standing position by pulling with his arms on two vertical handgrips. He is then held upright—the aid is essentially a body caliper.

footstools
A footstool can be used with a chair with a high seat if you need the extra height of the chair for getting up but find sitting in it uncomfortable because your feet do not touch the floor. The stool should be high enough to support the feet at a height which prevents pressure on the back of the thigh.

A footstool is, however, a hazard because it may be tripped over.

The stool must be pushed out of the way before getting up and replaced after sitting down. Castors on the stool make it easier to move it around. A stool with legs can be pulled into position with the handle of a walking stick hooked round a leg.

Some footstools are metal framed, with rubber ferrules for feet. An ordinary wooden stool is cheaper and has the advantage that its legs can be cut to the most comfortable height. If the top of a stool is slippery, it can be covered with a non-slip material.

leg rests
Leg rests are available in several different designs, with a variety of heights and angles. A leg rest must be long enough to support and raise the whole leg: the weight of the leg must not be taken through only the calf because this restricts circulation.

A leg rest may be needed by someone with swollen legs or ankles. But if you have swollen legs or ankles, you should consult a doctor.

Tables
The height of a table should relate to the height of a chair and the person in it. Ideally, when sitting, your elbows should be about level with the table top. The underneath height of the table is also important. There should be an adequate distance—say, about eight inches— between the chair seat and the under surface of the table so that the thighs are not compressed.

A table should be solid and firm because you may need to push on it to get up from the chair or use it for support as you cross the room. It should also be possible to draw the chair close to the table easily. Some tables have cross bars just above the ground which can obstruct the feet.

cantilever tables
If you have to spend a considerable time sitting in an armchair or in bed, a table which goes over the lap is useful. There are many different models of cantilever table, with different shaped bases. The RICA report No 11 (May 1972) deals with bed/chair tables.

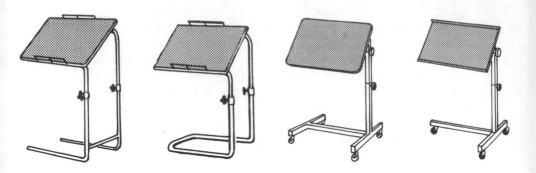

Chair legs make it impossible to slide a table with a U-shaped base into position and difficult with some H-shaped bases. A T-shaped base frame is less stable than other designs and the table may tip with a comparatively light load.

A height-adjustable table is more versatile than a fixed height type. When a table is to be used from several positions—from a chair, from a bed and as a book rest—you will probably want to be able to change its height. A table with a single pillar and a single tightening knob is easier to adjust than one with two pillars and two knobs.

There are various ways of fixing the table height. With the method of tightening one or two friction knobs, adjustment is more difficult and less safe for someone whose use of the hands is impaired. The easiest method for adjusting the height is by winding a crank handle. Some tables incorporate a safety stop to prevent raising the table top too far and pulling it off its base.

To provide a useful work surface, the table top should overlap the centre of a bed or chair by at least 8 inches (about 200 mm).

Many cantilever tables can be tilted to act as a book rest; with others, only part of the surface tilts. A table with a partially tilting surface eliminates the need to remove everything else from the table when you want to read. For supporting a newspaper, a large tilting surface is necessary. Other tables have a ledge to hold the book, and this can be uncomfortable if the table is used for writing.

Reading

Many local authorities provide a travelling library service. Some limit this service to people who are housebound and have no one who can change books for them. Large print books are available in most public libraries, and the range of titles is increasing. In some areas, the WRVS runs a books-on-wheels service in conjunction with the local library.

book rests

As well as being useful for someone who finds it difficult to hold a book, a book rest may help someone with poor eyesight to position a book at a convenient height and angle, and possibly in a better light.

There are book rests designed to stand on a table, others are floor standing similar to a music stand. Or a cantilever table can be used.

The type of book rest to choose depends on the situations in which it may be used. For someone who is going to sit up to a table, there are many small book rests to choose from, some of which adjust to different angles. Most fold away for storage. Someone who is going to read in a chair will be better off with a floor-standing frame, adjustable in height so that it can be used with any chair, and preferably with a top that can be tilted.

A book rest should be stable and not easily knocked over. If it adjusts in height or in angle, there must be sufficient adjustment to bring the book into the best position for the person reading.

The size of the books, magazines and newspapers likely to be read must also be considered when choosing a book rest. Some rests are unstable with anything heavy. The bigger rests take magazines, but most do not take a newspaper. A do-it-yourself adaptation for a newspaper can be made for a large book rest or a floor-standing frame by fixing two Klemmboy clips to the top of a board, placing the board on to the stand, and clipping the newspaper in position for reading. The newspaper will have to be pulled out and replaced every time to turn a page.

In the series *Equipment for the disabled,* the publication on *Communication* includes book rests among the aids described that help with reading and writing, and prismatic spectacles.

Someone who cannot sit up may need prismatic spectacles to see what is going on in the room, or read or watch television. These work rather like a periscope, and can enable someone who is lying down to see things at right angles to the eyes. Prismatic spectacles can be bought in opticians' shops, without a prescription or made up with lenses to your own prescription.

page turning
Someone with weak, numb or unsteady hands may have difficulty in turning the pages of a book. A pimple rubber thimble, or even two on adjacent fingers, may solve the problem. Paper clips can be used to separate the pages to make turning easier, but someone else has to fit the clips and they are inclined to tear the paper.

If you cannot use your fingers but have good control of the rest of your arm, you may be able to turn pages with the side of your hand or with your elbow, provided the book is lying flat. For someone who has lost the use of both hands, a headband with a unicorn-like thin angled rod firmly attached works well with forward pressure and a twisting head movement. A mouthstick can be used similarly. These devices must be fitted properly by a doctor or therapist, with the help of a dental technician for the mouthpiece.

Some severely disabled people may need an electrically operated page turner. Some can be operated by a micro-switch or a suck/blow mechanism.

The *Communication* publication in the *Equipment for the disabled* series also includes electric and manual or mouth page turners.

taped and filmed books

As well as the Talking Book Service for the Blind, there are various organisations which produce taped books on cassettes for the temporarily blind, the partially sighted or disabled people who cannot hold books. They usually charge an annual subscription for the use of tapes. The machine for playing the tapes can be hired; the local authority social services department may provide part or all of the cost.

The National Listening Library (49 Great Cumberland Place, London W 1H 7LH) provides taped books on cassettes for playing back on a machine designed so that the majority of handicapped people can operate it without difficulty. There is an annual subscription and the reproducing machine costs about £40.

The National Fund for Research into Crippling Diseases sells, or hires out, a microfilm projector which can be used from either a bed or a chair. This projects filmed books and is controlled by a pneumatic switch. It is particularly useful for technical books with diagrams and pictures which are an integral part of the text.

studying at home

For disabled or visually handicapped students, there are organisations which will tape any particular books for use on their machines.

The Open University system is specifically designed for the home-based student. The degree is built up out of a number of courses which may be taken over an extended period. It is possible to discontinue a particular course (perhaps because of ill health) and make a fresh start in a subsequent year. Where a student cannot attend a study centre, a student tutor and counsellor can keep in touch by letter, telephone or home visits. Additional counselling or tutorial sessions can be arranged for disabled students.

The Open University should be informed if a student's work is likely to be affected by health problems. Applicants who have any disability are asked to attach to their application form a letter outlining their difficulties (this will be treated as confidential). Enquiries should be addressed to the admissions office, The Open University, PO Box 48, Milton Keynes, MK7 6AB.

Writing

Anyone who has difficulty with writing should make sure of writing in a good position. It is usually easiest to write sitting up at a table, at a comfortable height. The chair should be near enough to the table to allow the forearm to be fully supported while writing. The pad should be moved farther on to the table as the page is filled up rather than moving the forearm towards the table edge.

It is easier to write on a large pad of paper rather than on loose sheets. There are various ways of stabilising paper. A clip board, obtainable from office equipment shops, will hold paper firmly, but the spring of the clip needs strong pressure to open it and help may be needed to insert the paper. A thin sheet of Dycem (non-slip double sided material) can be laid under the paper. Paper can be held down by small magnets or pieces of magnetic strip on a piece of metal sheet used as a writing board. Magnetic rulers are available and also rulers with a rubber strip to prevent the ruler sliding.

Felt tip pens and soft lead pencils need less pressure than other pencils and ballpoints. Giant pencils and large square-sectioned or triangular ballpoint pens may be easier to grip.

A pen or pencil can be made easier to grip by increasing its diameter, providing friction on the shaft, or making some kind of holder to supplement the gripping power of the fingers. Increasing the diameter can be done by wrapping foam rubber round the shaft, held with adhesive plaster.

A bigger hand grip can be made by inserting the pencil through a golf practice ball, a foam rubber ball or a block of foam rubber. The shaft can be made less slippery by twisting a rubber band round it or sticking on a piece of pimple rubber of the kind used on table tennis bats.

Weak finger muscles can be supplemented by knotting a wide flat rubber band round the pencil in such a way as to provide loops for thumb and forefinger. Another method is to make a strap which wraps round the fingers to stabilise the pencil. Provided there is sufficient overlap, the strap can be tightened round two, three or four fingers, whichever feels most comfortable.

Someone who suffers from severe tremor may be helped by wearing a weighted cuff. A cuff can be made by sewing a tube of strong cloth with compartments to take two or three pieces of lead. The cuff can be fastened to the wrist with velcro, positioning the pieces of lead so that they avoid the bony prominences on the wrist. This cuff can be useful in improving control not only of writing but also typing and eating.

—left-hand writing

Someone who has had a severe hand injury or a stroke may need to learn to write with the other hand. One way of doing this is to work through a good children's writing manual, starting with patterns to get the feel of the thing, and progressing to rows of similar joined letters before going on to words. Someone learning to write with the left hand should position the paper with the bottom right-hand corner opposite the middle of the body and the left-hand corner farther away from the edge of the table so that the pad is tilted about 30 degrees towards the right.

typing

It may be possible to manage a typewriter when writing is too difficult. An electric typewriter requires less effort to operate than a manual one and produces even type by whatever method it is operated and however uneven is the pressure exerted. IBM can sometimes supply reconditioned electric typewriters at a low cost to severely disabled people, such as spastics and people with multiple sclerosis or muscular dystrophy. But there is a very long waiting list.

When selecting a typewriter, check on the shape of the keyboard and the size and shape of the keys, and the accessibility and ease of operation of frequently used controls such as the paper feed. Someone who tends to hit two keys at a time may need a keyboard guard which can be fitted to some typewriters to prevent this.

A typewriter can be operated by a stick, attached to a mouthpiece. The mouthpiece should be made in consultation with a dental technician. Typewriters can be operated by the big toes, with a footboard to support the feet. For typing to be done when lying in bed, it may be necessary to make a wedge-shaped stand to fit on to a bed table to angle the typewriter forward so that it can be clearly seen. These adaptations can be made in an occupational therapy department or in the workshop of a special hospital unit for the severely disabled.

Special typewriter keyboard charts and instructions for handicapped typists, obtainable from the National Fund for Research into Crippling Diseases, gives charts for typing with just the left hand, just the right hand, and a series of charts on the fingering to use when the index, middle, ring or little fingers are missing on either hand. *Type with one hand* (obtainable from American Book Service, 57 Hill Avenue, Amersham HP6 5BZ) gives fingering charts and detailed instructions on typing with either hand.

A typewriter can be operated by a special Possum mechanism. This can be made available through the local authority or from the DHSS in a case of extreme difficulty in communication.

remote control equipment

Most of the remote control equipment designed for severely disabled people is both sophisticated and expensive, and specialised help will be needed to choose the most suitable equipment and adapt it to the person's requirements. With patient operated electronic selector mechanisms (Possum) it is possible to select and switch on and off up to 11 electrical devices. The person using the apparatus either depresses a microswitch or sucks on a pneumatic tube to operate the device. Possum control could include television channel change, alarm system, door entry mechanism with intercom, automatic curtain drawing, telephone answering and dialling. A Possum remote control system is expensive to buy; in some cases, it can be obtained through the national health service but only after careful assessment of the would-be user.

The Possum Users Association is run by users of Possum equipment for disabled people and those wishing to help them. The Association publishes a quarterly newsletter *Possability* for its members: the address is Copper Beech, Parry's Close, Stoke Bishop, Bristol BS9 1AW.

There are several other systems with varying methods of remote control. One has a light attached to a specially designed head band; the light beam is shone on to the control panel and by minimal head movements can be moved along it on to a typewriter keyboard or a control panel. It is not suitable for someone with any head tremor or involuntary movements. The light source can also be hand-held or attached to a foot.

With other systems, a microswitch or a sensor is activated by minimal muscular movements. A control panel lights up in sequence and the switch has to be activated to stop the light when it reaches the required function. Another system uses a special torch which can be focussed on a control panel from any position across a fairly large room.

Speaking

Anyone with a speech problem should consult a speech therapist. Speech therapists are employed by the area health authority and work in hospitals and in special clinics. But there is a grave shortage of speech therapists. To find out if there is a speech therapist working locally, ask your general practitioner or the area health authority. If they cannot help, write to the College of Speech Therapists, 47 St John's Wood High Street, London NW8 7NJ to ask where you can find one. Even if it is not possible to arrange for a series of treatment sessions, a consultation with a speech therapist can provide valuable advice on how to help overcome speech problems.

For someone who for mechanical reasons is unable to speak, writing everything down is a solution but this is slow and is only effective when communicating with one or perhaps two other people. The Lightwriter is a form of typewriter which produces a lit-up line of capital letters. This faces away from the typist so that several people can read it at the same time. As new characters are typed in, they displace the previous ones. There is a buzzer so that if the typist wants to join in the conversation, he presses the buzzer to indicate he is beginning to type. The Lightwriter is battery-operated and weighs just over 5 lb (2 kg).

Sometimes it is not only the ability to speak which is lost but also the ability to read or to recognise letters, or understand fully what is said. The degree of disability varies from person to person, and so does the ability to recover. It is not always for want of trying. Anyone who has a speech problem will need plenty of help from friends and relatives, even if lucky enough to be having speech therapy. *Without Words*, a pamphlet issued by the College of Speech Therapists, gives practical advice on how to help. A book *A stroke in the family* by Valerie Eaton Griffith (published by Wildwood House) describes how an actress managed to learn to speak again after a stroke, and explains how someone can be helped to recover speech.

Scrabble can be used as a therapeutic game and as a means of communication for someone who has some ability to read and understand words but who has a major difficulty in speaking. A spelling board with letters of the alphabet and numerals and some common words could be used with a pointer for basic communication. A word and picture chart published by the Chest and Heart Association (Tavistock House North, Tavistock Square, London WC1H 9JE) can be used to communicate basic needs such as 'hot drink', 'cold drink', 'glasses', 'bedpan'. The CHA also sell a series of 7 cassettes, *Learning to speak again after a stroke,* which can be used under the guidance of a speech therapist.

Sewing and knitting

The foot pedal switch of an electric sewing machine can be adapted for use by other parts of the body, and so can a knitting machine.

Electric scissors are available, both mains-operated and battery-operated, which are useful for someone who has weak or limited hand or wrist movement. So are Stirex scissors which have a loop spring at the end of the handle that can be operated like sugar tongs by inward pressure of the fingers; they have to be ordered through a social worker.

Anyone who has difficulty in threading a needle can buy a needle threader or use self-threading needles. These can be bought at most haberdashery shops.

Large print knitting and crochet patterns are available in the 'easy read' range of Wendy patterns.

Playing cards

Someone who has the use of only one hand or who has weak grip or limited finger movement, may find it difficult to hold playing cards. If the lid of a chocolate box is placed upside down on the table with the box inside it, the slit between the lid and the box will hold the cards. A handyman could make a more elegant holder by fixing two strips of perspex with a small space between into a strip of wood. A nylon scrubbing brush upside down can also be used for holding cards by putting them between the bristles.

For those who cannot easily shuffle cards, there is a card-shuffling device which can be operated with one hand. There are books describing some of the many versions of games of patience.

Picking-up devices

A pick-up stick or reaching aid enables a wide variety of objects to be picked up from the floor or from beyond reach on tables and shelves. It can also be useful for other activities such as switching on the light, drawing curtains, operating window catches and even for pulling on pants and stockings. But you may not need a special pick-up device: a reversed walking stick can be used to pick up a handbag or hook round a chair leg to move it, a book may be picked up in a long-handled dustpan, a magnet on a string can retrieve hairpins.

Individual requirements vary, and there are different designs of picking-up devices: outsize scissors, extending tongs, sticks with a lever at one end to operate sprung jaws at the other end.

The RICA comparative test report No 8 (July 1971) on pick-up sticks found that four of the ones tested were unsatisfactory, mainly because they were too difficult to use. It is therefore advisable, if at all possible, to try out a device before buying.

With most picking-up devices, the jaws are normally open and the user has to squeeze them closed round the object and keep up this pressure while lifting the object to a convenient place. One model of the Helping Hand has an additional lever that locks the jaws round the object so that it is held firmly until the lever is released. The lever handle on some pick-up sticks is easier to squeeze than on others. With some models, the lever opens so wide that an impossibly large hand span would be needed to close it with one hand.

The right length of pick-up stick depends mainly on whether you are going to use it most when sitting down or when standing up. With a shorter stick, less effort is required to pick things up and it is also easier to control the lifting process. Some manufacturers produce pick-up sticks in a variety of lengths; their longer models are slightly heavier. The weight of a pick-up stick must be considered, especially a long one where the stick has to be brought up through the horizontal position to a convenient height and will therefore feel heavier.

Someone with weak muscles needs a lightweight device but someone with strong arms and hands could manage one that gives the reach to pick up large and heavier objects. The width to which the jaws of a picking-up device open determines the size of objects which can be lifted. Those with the widest jaws tend to be the heaviest.

A pick-up stick with the handle at an angle of about 45° to the shaft is likely to be more comfortable than one with a straight handle. This is because the wrist can be kept straight if the handle is angled.

Several pick-up sticks have a magnet either on the jaws or on the handle. This is useful for picking up pins, needles and other small ferrous objects. It is more convenient if the magnet is at the jaw end because when it is at the handle end, the stick must be turned right round to use it.

You may want a picking-up device which you can carry about with you. There is a folding version of the Helping Hand, reducing it to $12\frac{3}{4}$ inches (320 mm), which means it can just about fit into a large pocket or capacious handbag.

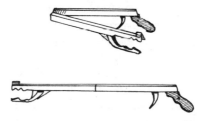

Lazy Tongs, which are like a piece of metal trellis, contract and can go inside a pocket or handbag. They are not particularly easy to use because the gap of the jaws depends on how far the lattice is extended. These tongs are more suitable for lifting soft objects such as a handkerchief or a ball of wool, not bigger solid objects such as a book. Someone who is at all uncoordinated may find them difficult to use.

A pick-up stick can be attached by two spring clips to a walking stick or a walking frame. A wheelchair user could keep a pick-up stick either tucked down the side of the chair or held in a clip alongside.

The ability to get about is limited for many elderly people by the state of their feet. Painful feet can be very disabling. Corns, hard layers of skin, bunions and toe deformities are largely the result of the wearing of ill-fitting shoes. It is important that shoes give good support and are comfortable; the temptation to wear soft slippers should be resisted because they do not give sufficient support, and if worn down are a hindrance to walking properly.

chiropody
Inability to cut the toenails increases discomfort. Soaking the feet for a time in hot water may soften the nails sufficiently to make cutting easier. But difficult nails should not be cut by an unskilled person. Regular chiropody may be needed.

A chiropody service has to be provided for everyone over pensionable age (free for those getting a supplementary pension) and for anyone registered as handicapped with the local authority. The chiropody service is the responsibility of the area health authority; in some areas it is run by a voluntary organisation. Your general practitioner or a social worker from the social services department should be able to give you information about getting chiropody. It may be possible for someone who cannot get out to a chiropody clinic to be visited at home by the chiropodist. Some areas are so short-staffed that the chiropody service is almost non-existent.

If you want to go to a chiropodist privately, the Society of Chiropodists (8 Wimpole Street, London W1M 8BX) will supply addresses of registered chiropodists in private practice.

handrails
Rails help someone who walks with difficulty or is unsteady to be safer and more independent at home. A handrail must be firmly fixed to the wall with long screws. A competent person should do this. *Handyman Which?* published a report on fixing things to walls in February 1974.

The best place to put handrails depends on the layout of the home and your particular handicap, which also determines the most suitable shape and size. Where possible, an occupational therapist should be asked to come and assess the problem.

It may be helpful to fix a handrail along a corridor or a handgrip at a step between rooms. Metal D-shaped handles are inexpensive and easy to fit. For example, one could be screwed to the front door frame to hold on to when unlocking the door.

walking sticks

The best length for a stick depends on what it is used for. To take weight off a painful leg, the stick should not be too long: a good length is level with the wrist crease when the arm is by the side. To help give balance to someone who is unsteady, it is safer to have two longer sticks to be placed well in front as you walk. It is possible to buy metal sticks which are adjustable in height.

Walking sticks come in different weights—heavy, medium and light. A stick should be stout and firm, not thin and whippy.

A straight horizontal handle on a stick gives good support but for some people may be uncomfortable because it forces the wrist to bend too far. A traditional curved handle may allow the wrist a more comfortable position.

A folding walking stick may be useful for someone who does not need a stick all the time. Using a stick at a bus stop or during the rush-hour ensures a degree of consideration from other people, even if you do not need the stick for just walking down the road.

When a walking stick is used because one leg is not functioning as it should, the stick should be held at the side opposite the weaker leg (not as if it were a crutch to prop up the bad side). This encourages the normal walking pattern of moving the opposite hand and leg together.

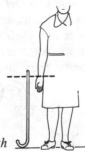

marking a stick for sawing it to the correct length

—ferrules

A stick should always have a rubber end or ferrule on the bottom to grip the ground.

Ferrules come in various designs. A plain smooth-ended ferrule tends to slip and should not be used. A suction tip grips the road better than a ferrule made of pimpled rubber, and lasts longer. A crutch tip with a flexible neck grips the ground whatever the angle of the stick.

There are different sizes, and the one with the biggest road-gripping surface that will fit the stick should be chosen. To hold a ferrule on to a thinnish stick, it may be necessary to wrap sticking plaster round the end of the stick before fitting the ferrule on.

Some people dislike being seen with a stick but will go out with a man's umbrella. This should be fitted with a rubber ferrule, and may need rather a lot of sticking plaster round the tip of the umbrella under the ferrule to keep it on.

A ferrule becomes slippery if it gets clogged with dust or mud, and should therefore be kept clean. When a ferrule gets worn down, it should be changed for a new one because it is no longer safe, and will be particularly dangerous in the wet. A ferrule will last longer if it is rotated from time to time; this prevents it wearing down at one side only.

Larger chemists and walking stick shops sell ferrules. Some local authority social services departments stock them. Patients may obtain ferrules free of charge from the hospital's physiotherapist or occupational therapist, or the appliance officer.

—stick holders

A terry clip, available from any hardware shop, can be screwed to the side of a chair or table so that a stick or crutch can be kept ready to hand. Alternatively, a magnet can be attached to the edge of the table and a terry clip or band of ferrous metal put round the stick.

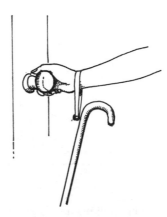

An elastic loop round a walking stick handle with a bigger loop to go round the wrist, or a leather thong fixed to the handle, leaves the hand free to grasp a rail or door handle without dropping the stick. But you must be very careful if grasping a banister rail that the dangling stick does not get in the way of your legs or caught in the stair rails. Alternatively, the stick could be hooked over the top button of a jacket or into a breast pocket, or hung over the crooked arm. It is sometimes useful to keep an extra stick or other walking aid at the top of the staircase, held with a clip.

other walking aids
If you need a more supportive aid than a stick, you should ask your general practitioner to refer you to the local hospital's physiotherapy department or if your local authority has a well developed occupational therapy department, you can go there. The therapist will assess your need, advise on choosing the correct walking aid for you and help you to learn how to use it most effectively—indoors, on the stairs and outdoors.

It is a good idea for a relative to go, too, to learn how best to give assistance with walking. A helper often tries to give more physical support than is needed. Grasping someone firmly by the arm may make walking more difficult because this disturbs the normal rhythm of body movement.

The walking aid may be a stick with three or four legs at the bottom, or a walking frame, or even crutches.

Crutches are designed to carry much more of a person's weight than a walking stick. For a crutch to be effective, it must not only take the weight off the feet but do so in such a way that the part of the body that presses on the crutch can take the strain. It is important for the physiotherapist to select the most suitable design of crutch, adjust it so that it is the correct length and the handgrip is in the best position, and teach you the best way of walking with the crutches.

A stick with three or four widely splayed legs (a tripod or a tetrapod) is much more stable than an ordinary walking stick. The number of legs is less important than having the centre of gravity falling inside the base. The stick can be stood on its own ready to use while you are sitting in a chair or opening a door. But it may be too wide to be used on the stairs.

—walking frames
Walking frames are very stable and help to give a feeling of confidence. But they do take up a lot of room and this may lessen their usefulness in the average home.

Some frames are rigid. The user picks up the frame, takes a step and puts the frame down again. In other words, it is humped along at each step, and is always there to act as a pulpit to lean on when needed. Other frames have wheels and can be tilted to push along.

What is called a reciprocal walking frame is something like a three-sided clothes horse, but lower. The user stands, holding on to both side pieces, as with any other walking frame. The frame is hinged, so it is possible to press down on one side piece for support and at the same time to lift the other side piece just clear of the ground and move it forward, taking a step with that leg at the same time. This is repeated with the other side of the frame and the other leg. This is much the same pattern of movement as walking with two sticks, but the frame gives more support. The hinges allow it to go through narrower places than a rigid frame.

Some walking frames fold so that the frame can be stored flat when not in use or put in a car.

The Pennyweight walking frame slides on its castors and can be braked by pressing down on the frame. It can be used when climbing up steps.

The Manoy walking aid is a lightweight frame mounted on two swivel castors and two nylon skids and is adjustable in height. It comes fitted with either hand grips or forearm supports. It has a basket, and also an angled perch seat for sitting for a short time at a work surface or for having a brief rest while walking round the house.

—trolleys

Walking with two sticks or crutches or a walking frame makes it difficult to carry things around the house. A stout trolley can serve a double function as a walking aid and carrying aid. The trolley must be strong, with a handle at the right height for you, and easy to guide. It should be fitted with reliable castors so that it steers easily; the castors need to be cleaned and oiled regularly.

The Etwall wooden trolley has a high handle which makes pushing easy, and the shelves are open at one end for sliding things on and off.

A plain wooden chair can be fitted with ballbearing castors on the legs and used as a walking and carrying aid if there is not sufficient room for a trolley or if there is no need to carry much at one time.

The Haven trolley aid is a rigid frame on castors, with a small removable top tray and, below, a further recessed trough for carrying things.

The Walkabout trolley can be used both indoors and out of doors. It has front castors and rear wheels with brakes and can be folded to fit into a car boot. Because of the position on the handle of the bar for the brakes, care must be taken not to trap the fingers.

A shopping basket on wheels can be useful, but does not give much support for walking. A shopping basket with four wheels, especially when it is full, gives more support than the type with two wheels and a front stabiliser. Using an old pram for shopping can be a help, although it may look odd.

An ablebodied housewife may get by without efficient planning or good work methods and even without good equipment. For the disabled housewife, however, these things may be essential and after the onset of a disability the habits of a lifetime may have to be reviewed, and existing implements adapted or new equipment bought. *Cleaning Equipment* published by the Disabled Living Foundation is a guide to choosing equipment for the physically handicapped.

A tidy, sparsely furnished room is more easily and more quickly cleaned than one with clutter. Pieces of furniture should be placed so that it is easy to clean round them. A couple of inches may make all the difference: for instance, the end of a bureau may be far enough from a wall to allow dust to collect in the gap but just not far enough to take a broom or vacuum cleaner. Furniture which has to be moved regularly while cleaning should be fitted with castors.

When new furniture is being bought, both its weight and its design should be thought of in practical as well as aesthetic terms. Some people need heavy and stable furniture for holding on to, others are glad to have light pieces for ease of moving and cleaning. Clearance under a piece of furniture should be sufficient for cleaning without getting down on all fours.

Planning your method of work helps. Getting together all the cleaning equipment that may be needed for a job rather than going back to fetch each item as it is required, cuts down the work. A shopping trolley, kitchen trolley or a walking aid trolley may be useful for this. An overall or an apron with large pockets or a bag which can be slung across the shoulders can be used to carry small equipment such as dusters and polish. Keeping an extra set of cleaning materials upstairs saves journeys up and down the stairs. Large equipment such as a vacuum cleaner should, if possible, be carried up or down stairs to where it will be needed the next day by another member of the household, or an ablebodied visitor.

Housework should be planned in advance to spread the heavier work evenly throughout the week and to allow plenty of time for all jobs. It is sensible to take frequent short rests during the work, and allow time afterwards for a longer rest. It is also wise to look out for labour-saving products; new ones are continually coming on the market.

There are usually some jobs that a housewife enjoyed before the onset of her disability or increasing age, and others that she disliked. If possible, she should continue to do the jobs she liked—for example, cooking—even if she takes a long time over it, leaving other jobs which she would now dislike more than ever, to others.

When help is provided by someone else, it should be worked out between you how much help is needed and who should do what. If a disabled housewife is given too much help, she may opt out of taking responsibility and becomes passive and dependent. On the other hand, it is wrong to allow someone with, for example, painful joints, to become over-fatigued by trying to keep up the appearance of being independent.

Home helps

A home help is someone employed by the local authority to go and help in the homes of people who cannot manage on their own. A home help is sent from the social services department usually on the recommendation of the doctor or a health visitor or social worker. The home help organiser visits first to discuss what help is needed.

The number of hours a week a home help comes depends both on the needs of the individual and on the facilities provided by the particular local authority. Some people are given help one or two hours a week, others maybe three hours three times a week, and some authorities provide a help seven days a week for a severely handicapped person. Sometimes there is a waiting list for any help at all. Depending on financial circumstances, a charge for this service may be made.

A home help is meant to do the housework, usually with the exception of work that involves climbing because of insurance if she should fall. This may mean that jobs like window cleaning and rehanging curtains will not be done. In addition to housework, a home help may go shopping and help with preparing meals. The home help organiser from the social services department can be approached at any time should the situation change and additional help or some other service be needed.

Cleaning floors
Uncarpeted floors should not be polished where there is an elderly or disabled person in the household. Most floors can be given a sealed finish that has a built-in shine and requires no more than a wipe over with a damp mop to keep it clean. A fitted carpet can be alternately vacuumed and swept with a carpet sweeper.

carpet sweepers
Sweepers are lighter and cheaper than a vacuum cleaner, and have the added advantage of not having to be plugged into a possibly inaccessible socket. A smaller carpet sweeper is easy to push, but it has to be pushed farther to cover the same area.

The handle of a carpet sweeper should be long enough so that there is no need to stoop when pushing it. It should be designed so as not to fall over when left in the upright position. Some carpet sweepers have handles composed of metal tubes that slot into each other: a short person or someone in a wheelchair can remove one section to make a shorter handle.

Some carpet sweepers are designed to work on either carpet or a floor. It is important that the floor/carpet lever that adjusts the height of the brushes can be easily operated.

Before buying a sweeper, check whether you can manage the pan-emptying mechanism. The smaller the sweeper, the more frequently it will need emptying.

vacuum cleaners
The upright type of vacuum cleaner requires less bending and causes less back strain; it can act as a walking aid, which makes it easier to move around the house than a cylinder type. But fitting the various attachments for other jobs, such as cleaning furniture or curtains, may well be more difficult than with a cylinder cleaner. Cylinder vacuum cleaners are more convenient for cleaning under furniture and into awkward corners. The nozzle of a cylinder provides maximum suction only if it is making contact with the floor at the correct angle, and this may be a problem for someone with weak grip or limited movement. An upright cleaner automatically assumes the correct angle.

When buying a new vacuum cleaner, it is important to consider the weight, especially if it has to be carried around the house. The method of emptying is also important. Some cleaners are easier and cleaner to empty than others, and some need emptying less frequently.

There is a RICA report on vacuum cleaners (September 1971, No 10 in the disabled user series).

brooms and brushes

For someone working one-handed, a shorter than usual broom may be useful because the broom head will be nearer and easier to control. Another method is to fit a broom with an aluminium gutter to take the forearm, and a short handle made from 1-inch (25 mm) dowelling

projecting at right angles to make a hand grip, in a similar way to an elbow crutch. (This adaptation can be used for other long-handled tools, such as a garden rake.)

A soft brush with bristles which fan out at the edges under slight pressure will sweep farther into corners and closer to furniture. One with rubber round the broom head avoids damaging the furniture or skirting board if the broom knocks against it.

A dustpan and brush with long vertical handles (the brush handle a little longer than the pan handle) saves having to kneel or stoop towards the ground. The balance of the dustpan should be such that the lip of the pan is in close contact with the floor even when the pan is standing on its own and that the handle stays upright. It is helpful if the dustpan and brush can be easily carried in one hand. Some dustpans have a tubular handle, into which the handle of the brush slides.

dry and wet mops

A long-handled mop with a flexible section to the handle is useful for cleaning underneath furniture without bending or from a wheelchair. Using this mop requires some strength in the hand and arm. These mops are often made with pivoting or revolving heads, which makes dusting round chair legs and into difficult corners easier.

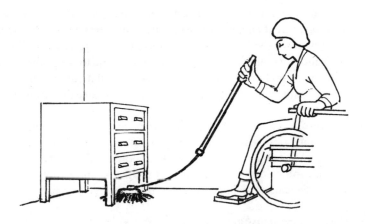

To avoid having to get down on hands and knees to scrub the floor, a long-handled sponge mop can be used or a long-handled scrubbing brush. A plastic bucket for the water will be lighter and therefore better than a metal one. The bucket can be filled by a hosepipe from the tap or with a plastic jug to avoid having to lift it out of the sink when full. It can be emptied by using a plastic jug, too. If the bucket that is used is just wide enough for the mop head to rest on the bottom, the bucket need not be filled more than a quarter to a half full. The traditional metal mop-wringing bucket for an oldfashioned cotton wet mop is heavy to move about and to empty. A small trolley can be made for moving a bucket by putting castors on to a platform or box so that it can be pushed along.

Some squeeze mops require an excessive amount of pressure to get the mop more than partially dry. With some, the squeeze mechanism is too low down the handle and you have to bend to reach it. Squeezing out a mop one-handed is not too difficult if the long handle is gripped under the good arm. Wrapping a length of non-slip material such as plastic foam round the handle where it rests under the arm will help to grip it tightly.

Using a window-cleaning mop avoids having to climb up on to something, or to lean out, to clean a window. These mops have a plastic foam head, usually adjustable in angle, on an extension handle; some have a rubber scraper at the back of the head. These mops can also be used for cleaning painted surfaces that are out of reach.

Dusting and polishing

A dusting mitt impregnated with polish or a small cotton mop impregnated with dust-absorbing liquid on a short plastic handle is effective at attracting and getting rid of dust.

If dusting is a problem, some attempt should be made to reduce the number of items to be dusted. Ornaments and books can sometimes be transferred to a glass fronted cupboard where they will stay clean for much longer.

A cobweb duster—a small brush at the end of a long, lightweight flexible pole—or a feather duster on a long handle, can be used for dusting inaccessible places.

Aerosol spray furniture polish takes a lot of the work out of polishing furniture. A thin film of polish is sprayed on and then rubbed off with a soft cloth. This removes dust and sticky marks, and leaves a polished surface without the need for hard rubbing.

A wheelchair can be provided free under the national health service through Department of Health and Social Security appliance centres. The chair must be recommended by a doctor who fills in a form (AOF 5G) giving details of the person's disability and the type of chair required. The doctor may call in an occupational therapist or physiotherapist to assess which chair would be most suitable. This assessment may be done at a wheelchair clinic and ideally should be associated with a home visit to look at the environment in which the chair will be used. This is particularly important if the person will be using the chair continuously. Further help in choosing a chair may be sought from the DHSS appliance centre who may send a technical officer to sort out particularly difficult problems. The appliance centre takes the final decision on which chair is supplied and makes the necessary arrangements. There are about 30 artificial limb and appliance centres in the UK.

More than one wheelchair may be supplied if medically recommended: for example, a transit chair to take in the car and an electric wheelchair for use inside the house. If a second wheelchair is required solely for use at work, this may be supplied by the Department of Employment on permanent loan.

The DHSS provides a far bigger range of chairs than any one manufacturer. The Department provides a chair from the range made under contract for the DHSS, unless there are very good medical reasons why one of these chairs is unsuitable. The DHSS will change a chair for a different model if it becomes unsuitable. A standard wheelchair can be provided with additional and alternative items, such as a different seat size, to suit an individual's needs. Such adaptations would cost a great deal on a privately bought chair.

Buying a wheelchair privately almost certainly means acquiring a smart chromium-plated chair. But it will not necessarily be more suited to the person's needs. Many manufacturers are not interested in supplying specially adapted chairs. Those who do, charge quite a lot of money to cover the extra expense. Adaptations should be ordered with the chair; work done later will spoil the finish of the chair. Some adaptations are not possible on chromium-plated chairs because chrome cannot be welded. And apart from the initial expense of buying a chair, regular maintenance and replacement are costly.

If a wheelchair is wanted for a short period only, for use on holiday or for someone who has a temporary disability, it is usually possible to borrow a chair from the social services department of the local authority or hire one from the local branch of the St John Ambulance Brigade or the Red Cross. There will probably be a limited range of chairs available, and for a loan during the holiday season, a booking should be made well ahead. There are also firms that hire out chairs on a weekly or monthly basis. Anyone who needs a chair for regular use should not keep a borrowed chair but should have one recommended to suit his individual requirements.

Self-propelled wheelchairs
Self-propelled wheelchairs are propelled by pushing the large wheels round with your hands on a handrim. They can also be pushed from behind by someone else.

A self-propelled wheelchair is not just a mobile piece of furniture. It will be used for many activities as well as for getting about. A wheelchair must not only be the best chair for your physical limitations but must be suitable for use in your home. A chair that is too wide to go through the doorways will be of no use. When the occupational therapist visits the home first, she measures the doorways, the height of the bed, the dimensions and turning spaces in the bathroom and lavatory and corridors, and any steps and stairs.

choosing the chair
It is almost impossible to get all the desired features combined in one wheelchair. For example, a chair designed for maximum manoeuvrability does not have maximum stability. A chair of minimum weight which folds up as small as possible for transit is not maximally robust, and may not be very comfortable.

There are at least a dozen points to consider before deciding on a chair—whether you are buying it yourself or getting it supplied by the Department of Health.

—width
Most self-propelled wheelchairs vary in width from 22 inches to 26

inches (560 mm to 660 mm). The entrance to some lifts and public
lavatories is only 24 inches (610 mm) wide, and houses have even
narrower doorways or corridors. It is usually best to have the
narrowest wheelchair that will be comfortable even when wearing
outdoor clothing. This will give good side support, which is important
when the trunk muscles are weak. It also enables a straight downward
push of the arms for propelling, which is easier than holding the arms
outwards and pushing down. But too narrow a wheelchair for your
body weight will not be stable and may therefore tip over on an even
surface.

For some chairs, a wheelchair-narrower to reduce the width of a
chair temporarily when going through a doorway is available. This
consists of a winding mechanism which draws the two sides of the
chair together, and can be operated by the person sitting in the chair. It
can only be used on some collapsible chairs not fitted with a cushion
with a rigid base.

A do-it-yourself wheelchair narrower can be made from a small,
high-ratio, block and tackle pulley; details are available from the
Disabled Living Foundation.

As a temporary narrower, a metal bar with both ends bent downwards at right angles can be fitted across the bottom members of a
wheelchair. This can only be fitted or removed when the wheelchair is
not occupied. It would be useful, for example, for negotiating a narrow
bathroom door for someone who only baths once a week.

—depth
The depth front to back of a wheelchair seat is important. A small
person may find the standard seat too deep. When sitting upright in a
chair, with the back firmly supported, there should be a space of about
two inches between the front of the chair seat and the back of the knee.
It may be necessary to use a back cushion to achieve a comfortable
depth. Junior sized chairs are often suitable for small adults, and
usually have a shallower seat.

—seat height
Wheelchairs vary in height from 17 to 20 inches (about 430 mm to

5 10 mm). The seat height of a wheelchair should be as near as possible to the height of the bed, lavatory or commode to which it may be necessary to transfer. If you are able to stand up, pivot and sit down again, the height is less critical, but for sliding sideways off the chair, it is important. Since not all surfaces will be at the same height, it may be necessary to adjust the height of, for example, the bed or lavatory. An extra thick cushion in a standard chair may be a better answer than a specially high chair. But too thick a cushion may make it difficult to reach the wheels for propelling.

—cushions

A cushion is an extra. The doctor has to order one, if required, from the DHSS when recommending a patient for a chair. Sitting for long periods without a cushion may be uncomfortable. Wheelchair cushions vary in thickness from 1 to 4 inches (about 25 mm to 100 mm), and the depth should be considered in relation to the required height of the seat and the arm rests.

If you are going to transfer from your wheelchair to a bed, bath, lavatory or car by sliding sideways along a transfer board, a cushion is helpful so that the transfer board will bury itself into the cushion's surface.

Sitting on a deep soft cushion can further immobilise a severely disabled person. A cushion with a plywood base gives firmer support when the wheelchair seat is pvc-coated fabric slung between two bars. A paraplegic cushion, with a U-shaped cutout to take a urinal, needs a hard base because a soft cushion may collapse into the middle and cover the urinal.

Most cushions are made from foam rubber covered by some non-absorbent material, and some people find them uncomfortably warm and damp. A fabric-covered cushion can be ordered instead.

There is a particular danger of pressure sores developing when someone cannot use his arms to ease the weight off the buttocks and change position frequently. Special cushions are available. With ripple cushions, which look rather like a miniature li-lo, an electric pump pushes the air through a series of alternating tubes: first one set of ridges is blown up and takes the pressure of the body, then these collapse and the ridges between them inflate, relieving the pressure from one skin area and transferring to another. Gel cushions contain a gelatinous substance which adapts to the contours of the body and distributes the weight evenly. Cushions filled with polystyrene granules adapt in a similar way. Some people find sitting on a medical sheepskin is comfortable and relieves pressure, others find it too hot.

—arm rests

Arm rests may be fixed or detachable. You need detachable arm rests if you are going to transfer sideways from the chair. Most detachable arm rests have catches to hold them firmly in position when attached.

The height of the arm rests may be critical. If they are too low, they give inadequate side support to someone with poor balance. If they are too high, they may rub against the arms when propelling the chair. If they are at the wrong height, they will not provide a comfortable place to rest the arms. Using a cushion to increase the seat height can make the arm rests too low: the depth of padding on the arm rests should be increased or taller arm rests fitted.

The standard type of arm rest extends almost to the front of the seat. With a well-fitting chair, these give lateral support and provide good arm support when leaning forward from the chair. They also provide support on which to push when standing up. Some people do not need arm rests at all, and this lessens the weight of the chair.

What are called domestic arm supports are cut away at the front to allow closer access to a table or desk. The DHSS will issue a pair of this type as an alternative or in addition, if necessary.

—foot support

The distance between the foot rests and the seat is usually adjustable over a range of about 5 inches (about 130 mm). The foot rests should be positioned so that the thighs are in a horizontal position on the seat when the feet are placed firmly on the rest.

It is most useful if the foot rest is easily detachable or retractable or each foot plate can be hinged upwards and out of the way by the person in the wheelchair. Some foot rests can only be detached by a helper, or by first getting out of the chair. Some foot rests need a spanner to detach them. Make sure this is supplied with the chair.

Clearance at the front of the chair is necessary when rising from the chair and also for getting close up to furniture which is solid to floor level, such as a kitchen unit. Moving or removing the foot rest reduces the overall length of the chair by about 9 inches (about 230 mm). This makes a great difference when going into a small lift or lavatory, or negotiating a narrow corridor.

A foot rest extension can be useful for someone who needs extra space for the feet but it reduces manoeuvrability by adding to the length of the chair.

Heel loops attached to the foot rests prevent the feet slipping back against the castors, especially when the chair is tilted. Toe loops prevent the feet falling forwards. Leg straps and panels against which the calf can rest support the leg and prevent a flaccid leg from falling off the foot rest.

Elevating leg rests of various types are available. These hinge from below the chair seat and can be raised to any chosen position up to the horizontal. It is unlikely that the person in the wheelchair can do this unaided. When the leg rest is up, the length of the chair is much increased, which may prevent it going round corners. Considerable weight is put on the leg rest and the adjusting mechanism tends to get worn and loose. An ordinary leg rest or even a footstool may prove less cumbersome and more satisfactory.

—the back

The back of a standard DHSS chair is angled at 15° from the upright. Chairs can be specially ordered with the back fixed at a suitable angle for you. Some chairs have an adjustable back rest, but this cannot be operated by the person in the chair.

A back extension is useful for someone with limited strength in the neck. A fully reclining back rest, combined with swinging elevating leg rests and a head extension, enables someone to lie back and sleep during the day without getting into bed.

Most wheelchairs fold for transit. The back needs to be hinged if the chair is to be stowed away in a car. Some methods of folding a chair are easier to manage than others. The therapist or the technician at the appliance centre should be asked to demonstrate how to fold the chair you are going to have. If you are going to take the chair into a car, you should practise to see if you can both fold and lift it in yourself.

—the propelling wheels

The wheels with which you propel a wheelchair are between 20 and 24 inches (about 510 mm to 610 mm) in diameter. The larger the wheels, the greater the leverage; nevertheless someone with limited arm movement would find smaller wheels less hard work. Someone with strong arms and good shoulder movement who uses a wheelchair out of doors may prefer a chair with larger wheels. A capstan handrim—eight 1-inch prongs fitted round the wheel—can be supplied with some types of chair. This enables you to push the wheel round with the palm or knuckles.

Someone with a weak back has more support while propelling in a chair with rear propelling wheels.

—rear propelling wheels

A chair with big back wheels has castors at the front. These castors are usually 5, 7 or 8 inches (130 mm, 180 mm, 200 mm approximately) in diameter. The small castors are good indoors but outdoors catch on bumps and kerbs and tend to tip the chair (castors with balloon tyres help to obviate this). A chair with small castors can be propelled backwards over rough ground. Large castors run over small obstacles more easily but are clumsy when manoeuvring in small spaces such as a lift, and because they protrude farther from the sides of the chair, they tend to jam against walls or furniture.

A chair with large rear wheels can be tilted on them to go up and down kerbs. Tipping levers to enable a helper to negotiate kerbs and steps are fitted.

Rear wheels which come below the level of the seat do not impede sideways transfer. Larger ones will be an obstacle and may only be suitable if you can take some weight on your feet when transferring. Big wheels fitted towards the back of a chair also allow room for foot rests to swing sideways out of the way so that the chair can be brought close to, for example, a lavatory.

Someone with no legs who does not wear artificial limbs may be given a chair with large wheels at the front to avoid the danger of the chair tilting backwards because of little weight at the front, but it may be better to have a chair with rear propelling wheels fitted about three inches farther back than usual to alter the centre of gravity.

—front propelling wheels

Wheelchairs propelled by big wheels at the front are easier to get over the edge of rugs and carpets and over uneven ground outdoors. The big wheels are in a more accessible position for someone with restricted movement in shoulder or elbow joints. When negotiating kerbs and stairs, because these chairs cannot tilt on their castors it is necessary to go down backwards. You cannot transfer sideways from this type of chair and the wheels at the front prevent close access to a working surface or piece of furniture.

Chairs with one castor at the back have a small turning circle, which makes them very manoeuvrable in a restricted area such as a kitchen, but are less stable. A chair with twin castors may be recommended for a tall heavy person because two castors give the chair more stability despite the bigger turning circle.

A chair with propelling wheels at the front is more awkward for a helper to push than one with the large wheels at the rear because it is difficult to steer.

—propelling with the feet or one hand

Wheelchairs can also be propelled by the feet. Someone who cannot use the arms to propel a wheelchair but has difficulty in walking may be able to manoeuvre a chair with 5-inch (about 130 mm) castors at the back and front and no big wheels. These chairs can be operated by walking with the heels, either pushing backwards or clawing forwards, or by punting with one or two walking sticks. Going backwards is usually easiest. Alternatively, a strong comfortable wooden chair can be fitted with four castors; the chair legs need to be shortened to allow the heels to reach the floor. Such a chair will go through places too narrow for other wheelchairs. The chair can be stabilised for getting out of by backing it against the wall or suitable furniture, or castors with brakes can be used.

One-hand drive chairs are available. A young person with one strong arm may be able to manoeuvre and steer such a chair (but will find it tiring over any distance). An elderly person recovering from a stroke will usually find it easier to propel a lightweight wheelchair with the good hand and use the good foot with a clawing-the-ground motion to keep it on course.

—tyres

Pneumatic tyres give a more comfortable ride for people who are in pain, and when travelling over rough ground. They provide better traction on wet and greasy pavements, and when mounting kerbs or steps, and reduce the overall weight of the chair. But pneumatic tyres have to be kept pumped up, and occasionally have a puncture. Anyone who is getting a chair with pneumatic tyres should ask for a pump at the same time. When they get soft, pneumatic tyres are difficult to propel.

Solid tyres make the chair easier to propel generally, particularly indoors on a smooth surface. They are best for a person with weak arms, or someone who would have difficulty with pumping tyres.

—brakes

There are brakes on wheelchairs to stop the chair from running away when you are getting in and out. It is possible to have brakes fitted which allow the chair to move forwards with a series of forward pushes but prevent it running backwards between pushes.

Extension levers for the brakes may make reaching them easier, but may interfere when you want to transfer sideways. Detachable brake extension levers are available for many chairs. Most brakes are operated by pulling backwards on the brake lever; some chairs have forward-operating brake levers. This can be confusing, especially for someone who has two chairs with different systems.

When both brakes are operated from one side, the cable tends eventually to stretch and then one wheel brakes less efficiently than the other.

Brakes and tyres should be checked regularly. Solid tyres gradually wear down, leaving the brakes less efficient unless they are adjusted to compensate.

—weight

The lightest weight chair on the market weighs about 30 lb (13·5 kg), some chairs weigh as much as 56 lb (25 kg). Weight depends not only on the material from which the frame of the chair is made but on the size of the castors, whether the chair has solid or pneumatic tyres, and the attachments. But having a slightly lighter chair will make little difference if the occupant weighs 16 stone (over 100 kg).

—extra attachments

A detachable table top that fits on to the front of the arm rests is useful for working and writing, and for meals. A table top may be a simple tray or a lap board shaped to fit within the chair, close to the body. The majority of DHSS wheelchairs have a fitting to take a tray. Some chairs can be fitted with various tops; for others a table top must be specially made.

Mobile arm supports can be attached to the back of a chair. These support the forearm, allowing it to move freely in the horizontal plane and also tip to allow the hand to reach down to a working surface and up to the mouth. They are activated by minimal movement and need careful fitting and expert adjustment. A gantry attached to the back of the chair to support the arm in a sling has a similar function. But a

gantry is unsightly and cumbersome, and does not provide as fine a control or wide a range of movement as mobile arm supports, and requires more effort to use.

getting the chair

You may have to wait for only a week for a standard chair but some months for a chair with special adaptations. The chair may be delivered direct to your home, folded for transit. The DHSS provide a booklet with every chair they supply, but when the wheelchair arrives you should get instructions from a therapist about using it: how to put on the brakes; how to remove the arm rest and transfer sideways; how to move the foot rests; how to put the chair into a car; how to be helped up steps and kerbs. The family should also be brought in and taught their part in getting the best use out of the chair.

When a wheelchair is first brought into a home, it is usually necessary to rearrange the furniture, and possibly remove some of it, to allow for the extra space the chair will need in use. If someone is going to be in a wheelchair permanently, it is pleasant to have a space kept for the chair in the sitting room where it can be part of the family circle.

A wheelchair will wear out a carpet quickly because it traverses the same routes over and over again. If you want to be able to replace parts of the carpet as they wear out, you could use carpet squares, which abut on to each other to form a smooth surface. Squares can be taken up and exchanged as they begin to get worn.

If it is necessary to widen a doorway in the house because it is too narrow to take the wheelchair (and a wheelchair-narrower cannot be used), this is the kind of modification that might qualify for a grant from the local authority.

—maintenance

A wheelchair should be properly maintained. Brakes should be checked regularly. Tyres wear out and need to be replaced. Maintaining a chair is similar to looking after a bicycle. Anyone who finds it difficult could ask a local bicycle shop to clean and oil the movable parts and check the chair over at least once a year.

If something goes wrong with a chair supplied by the DHSS, the chair should be returned to the appliance centre or hospital for repair or replacement. The Department of Health may lend you a wheelchair temporarily while your permanent chair is away being repaired.

After you have had your DHSS chair for three months, and thereafter every year, you receive a letter enquiring about the serviceability and suitability of the chair you have. You should reply whether or not the chair is working well, and report if it is not comfortable or is not fulfilling your needs. Do not be diffident about saying if a chair that was all right last year has becomes unsatisfactory for you. To get another DHSS chair, you may have to go back to the doctor who recommended you for a wheelchair, or to the appliance centre that supplied it. A technical officer from the appliance centre may come to visit you at home to assess the problem.

Pushed wheelchairs

If a chair is always going to be pushed, big wheels are both unnecessary and heavy. It is better to have four small wheels, or two small wheels and castors. Chairs with four wheels are difficult to steer round bends. Chairs with two wheels and two castors are difficult to steer in a straight line.

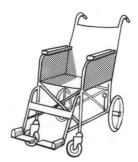

Most chairs for pushing being made nowadays are light in weight, can be folded out of the way and carried in a car. But there is a rigid wooden wheelchair for indoor use, supplied by the DHSS, which looks oldfashioned but is generally better upholstered than a canvas chair and is comfortable for sitting in for long periods. With one rear castor, it is very manoeuvrable. It can be fitted with a commode.

For outdoor use, there is the old fashioned type of chair with a pram handle, which has the advantage of being very well sprung and is therefore comfortable even when pushed a long distance. The pram handle helps the pusher to tilt the chair. The chair has a laced seat; this lacing should be kept tight, like shoe laces, to avoid sagging. The chair can be supplied with a waterproof apron.

A car transit chair which folds to go into the car is designed primarily for taking someone out to a car and to be there to transport the person when he arrives at his destination. It is not suitable for pushing for long distances or over soft or rough ground but could be useful to take a housebound disabled person to the nearby shops or to church.

A lightweight folding pushchair, the Buggy Major, is useful for a small light person who cannot walk far. This chair folds completely, like a golf trolley, and can easily be taken on public transport, but is not very robust.

There is a nylon carrying seat (the Trans-Sit seat) which can be lifted by handles like those at the side of a baby's carry cot. It needs two people for carrying. It can also be supplied with shoulder straps. This seat may be useful when a wheelchair is not practicable, such as getting on to a coach or an aircraft or down to the beach.

—*pushing*

Chairs with wheels at the back have a tilting lever at the rear of the chair. When going down a kerb or step, press down with the foot on the tilting lever, so that the front castors or wheels come off the ground, and lower the chair gently, keeping the back wheels in contact with the kerb until the wheels touch the ground. Do not push the wheelchair hard over the edge of the kerb because it will land with a bump. When climbing a kerb, use the tilting lever again to get the front castors on the pavement and push the chair forward so that the back wheels mount the kerb. If possible, choose the shallowest part of the kerb. When climbing two or more steps, it may be better to go up backwards.

Chairs with castors at the back do not have a tilting lever, so the chair must be pulled up a kerb backwards. Going down a kerb, the front wheels must be lowered gently over the edge.

It is important to understand the braking system and to make sure that the brakes are off when starting to push and are put on again safely when the chair has stopped.

The Red Cross have published an illustrated booklet *People in wheelchairs: hints for helpers*.

When wheeling a chair proves very difficult because the disabled person is heavy, the pusher is weak or the district is hilly, it is possible to get a power-assisted pedestrian-controlled wheelchair from the DHSS (but not in addition to a mobility allowance or if you have any other powered vehicle from the DHSS). It is also possible to buy a version of some powered chairs with the controls at the back, to be controlled by someone walking behind.

Powered wheelchairs

A powered indoor chair may be provided by the Department of Health and Social Security for someone who is not only unable to walk but also is unable to propel a wheelchair, on condition that this chair will help him to achieve some measure of independence at home or at work. This means that the person is assessed not only on his physical state but on his domestic environment. The DHSS are sometimes not too rigid on borderline cases. For instance, someone who can propel himself for short distances in a wheelchair may find this so exhausting that he is unable to achieve any other useful activity, and someone else who can propel a chair round the house without difficulty may find that in a residential centre, a special school or his place of work, he needs to propel himself over distances and slopes that are more than he can manage. A case for helping such a person achieve increased independence is best made out by a doctor who is familiar with what is available.

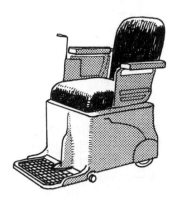

The DHSS's standard electrically propelled indoor chair (the Epic) is a solid, padded chair which looks somewhat cumbersome but is comfortable, very manoeuvrable and gives good support. It has easily operated controls and can have power-assisted steering. It has a built-in battery charger which saves time and trouble. If this particular chair is not suitable for someone whose need comes within the specified criteria, the Department of Health can supply an alternative from the range of powered chairs available.

Some powered chairs are designed solely for indoor use. They can be taken through french windows on to a flat terrace but are unable to negotiate gradients or obstacles. Some chairs, designed to be used both in the house and the garden, can negotiate small obstacles and reasonable gradients. Others are designed to be used in the house and garden and also to be taken out on the road. These can negotiate steeper gradients and either climb kerbs or carry portable ramps to bridge kerbs. Some chairs are designed primarily for road and garden use, can climb steep gradients and can even tow a garden barrow. They look more like mini tractors than wheelchairs, but even so some people use them indoors as well.

Some of the features that are good for an indoor chair are less good for an outdoor chair. Manoeuvrability is very important indoors.

Stability is more important out of doors. A chair with a short wheel-base, narrow track and good steering lock is very manoeuvrable. A chair with a long wheelbase, wider track and limited steering lock is more stable.

A disabled person is allowed to use a powered chair on public footpaths provided the chair does not exceed 250 lb (about 125 kg) in weight, is not capable of exceeding 4 mph and meets certain braking requirements. No driving licence is needed and the law does not require third party insurance for such a vehicle. Front and rear lights must be carried at night.

A stipulation for a powered chair supplied by the DHSS, however, is that it must not be used on the streets. If you want to use a powered wheelchair outside the curtilage of the house, you have to get one for yourself. (A voluntary organisation may be able to help with buying one.)

People who can propel themselves in a wheelchair may nevertheless feel that a power-driven chair would be an asset. Someone who likes going out into the countryside may find propelling a chair over bumpy fields impossible. A person who finds transferring from a chair to a car difficult may want to have a power-driven chair which he can use to go out to the local shops and to visit friends.

It is possible to buy conversion units which turn self-propelled wheelchairs into powered ones. Some of these conversion units fit on to only certain chairs, others can be adapted to be fitted on to most makes of wheelchair.

There is a drawback to changing to a powered chair. Propelling a wheelchair exercises the arms and keeps them strong. If you change to a power-driven chair, and therefore do not have to use your arms, transferring from the chair may become difficult or impossible because the arms have become weak. One solution may be to use a power-driven chair part of the time and a self-propelled chair as well, perhaps one indoors and one out.

Many of the features relevant to self-propelled wheelchairs apply also to the selection of a powered chair. There is far more variety in the overall design of powered chairs and new models are being produced and some older models withdrawn frequently. The information service of the Disabled Living Foundation can give information on the various powered chairs currently on the market. A severely disabled person who may have difficulty in controlling a chair should seek the advice of a doctor and therapist experienced in recommending powered chairs. No one should get a powered chair without trying it out first, preferably more than one to find the most suitable. The positioning of controls and the amount of effort and range of movement required to operate them will be critical. Chairs have been made to operate by single levers controlled by a finger, a toe, the mouth or even a suck–blow mechanism.

—steering

The steering on powered chairs is either manual or power-assisted. A severely disabled person may find power-assisted steering essential.

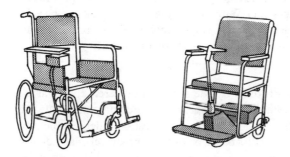

The controls of a chair are usually either mounted on one arm rest or on a steering column between the user's legs; they can be fixed almost anywhere else if necessary. When controls are on the arm rest, it is usually possible to choose which side to have them. A central steering column can either be lifted or pushed out of the way when getting in or out, but may be quite heavy to lift. Some people like the central stick control between their legs because they feel it prevents them falling out of the chair. Others, particularly women, find that it gets in the way and looks inelegant. The central control of one chair (the Batric) comes over the knees and so would not divide a skirt.

—brakes

A powered chair is normally braked by the drag of its motor, in the same way as when a motor car is left in gear. A chair which is taken out on to a public footpath must by law be able to hold its position on a 1 in 5 slope by direct mechanical action—that is, with the power switched off. Anyone who is buying a power-driven chair with the intention of taking it out on public footpaths should check this with the manufacturer first. Some chairs have conventional handbrakes as well. These are an additional safeguard, for example, when parking on a steep hill, but may require some strength to operate.

If a chair breaks down, it may be impossible to push because of the drag of the motor. This would be a problem if the chair broke down where there was no one able to lift the stranded user and get him home. On some of the chairs, the motor can be disconnected to allow the chair to be pushed (it has to be reconnected for braking or the chair wedged while the occupant gets out). With others, the control stick can be held in a freewheel position which is somewhere between 'braking' and 'slow speed'. This is another point to check before acquiring a chair.

—support

The amount of support given by the seat of a powered chair varies. Some models are similar to self-propelled wheelchairs, and some are available with an adjustable back rest, head rest, and detachable arm rests. The newer indoor chairs based on office-type swivel chairs do not give much support, and are suitable only for someone with good control of the trunk muscles. The chairs designed primarily for outdoor use are also generally not suitable for someone with weak trunk muscles, even with a retaining strap around the waist, but can be adapted by the manufacturer.

—manoeuvring

Manoeuvrability in a chair is usually more important indoors than out. The turning circle of some power-driven chairs is more than that of a self-propelled chair because they are longer and wider, but it is possible to cut this down by doing a three-point turn.

The gradients a chair can climb will partly determine where it can be taken out of doors. As a guide, a chair for indoor use may manage a gradient of 1 in 12, one suitable for the house and the garden 1 in 10, and one for use on public footpaths should be able to manage gradients of up to 1 in 6. The Batric can climb steeper gradients but the user needs to be able to lean forwards over the front to prevent the chair tipping over backwards.

Most power-driven chairs are unable to negotiate kerbs because they do not have the extra power required. In a self-propelled chair, you may be able to give the extra push to get a chair up a kerb, but an electric motor ticks over at a constant level. Moreover, some powered chairs have small wheels and it is easier to negotiate kerbs with large wheels. One powered chair is powerful enough to climb kerbs four to five inches high using the right technique—but it is inevitably a bumpy ride.

It is often possible to avoid kerbs by using slopes instead. You could use a pair of lightweight portable ramps to negotiate a kerb provided your trunk and arm muscles are strong enough to place the ramps in position and lift them up again.

Some local authorities are replacing kerbs with small ramps at crossings, mainly to help mothers with prams. It is worth approaching your local authority to ask if it will provide such a ramp at road crossings between your home and, for example, the nearest shops.

—speed and range
The speed of a powered chair is important if it is to be taken on public footpaths. If it goes too slowly—that is, at less than a slow walking

pace—it may take so long getting anywhere that it is not really practicable. If it exceeds 4 mph, to be legal it must be used on the road and not travel on the pavement. Indoor chairs usually have speeds of $\frac{3}{4}$ mph to 1 mph; chairs for use in the garden usually go up to 3 mph, and those for use on public footpaths up to $3\frac{1}{2}$ mph or 4 mph.

On the Newton E chair and the Vessa, the farther forward you push the control lever, the faster the chair goes.

All powered chairs in the UK are electric. They are powered by batteries which are recharged by a unit supplied with the chair. Some chairs are easier to recharge than others; some have a built-in recharging unit. A chair in constant use will need recharging every night. When a battery is getting flat or wearing out, the chair will manage only shallow gradients and the user may get stuck at the bottom of his garden.

The distance a powered chair can travel before needing recharging is important when taking it out of doors. Most people need a chair with a range of at least 3 miles, although this will depend on individual circumstances and local topography. The range of different makes varies considerably. There are chairs with a maximum of 4 miles, 6 miles, 8 miles, and even 12 miles—for example, the Batricar, a four-wheeler developed from the Batric powered chair.

Some powered wheelchairs can be folded or dismantled and transported in a small or medium sized car. Those that cannot be dismantled can only be transported in a large estate car, van or trailer. Powered wheelchairs are heavy to lift.

Powered chairs should be regularly serviced; this is even more important than with self-propelled wheelchairs. Chairs supplied by the DHSS have a routine inspection every year and are serviced at DHSS approved repairers. With a privately obtained chair, it may be worth sending the chair back to the manufacturer for a regular overhaul, or the local garage may be prepared to service it.

powered platforms

Another type of indoor powered chair now on the market is basically an office type chair on a powered platform which looks much more like a normal chair than the conventional wheelchair. But it is only viable on the level and must therefore be kept at the office or in the house. You would need another wheelchair to go outdoors, or even to go down a ramp. The Department of Health would be unlikely to supply one because for anyone sufficiently disabled to satisfy their criteria for a powered wheelchair, such a chair would be unlikely to be considered the most suitable to his needs.

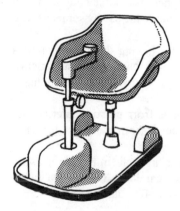

The Chairmobile consists of a three-wheeled powered platform with a steering column at the front which can be lifted out when getting on and off the chair. The motor is contained in a rather large hump between the user's feet, which makes getting on from the front and positioning the feet on the platform difficult for some people. The platform can be supplied with a fixed or adjustable swivel office type chair fitted to the platform or it can carry any chair or stool with back legs not exceeding $17\frac{1}{2}$ inches (about 440 mm) wide. Someone who is able to get on to a high stool can therefore talk to people at standing height, rather than having everyone bend down to speak to him. The Chairmobile moves at less than 1 mph and has a range of just over a mile. It turns in an arc rather than rotating on itself.

Wheelchair accessories

Anyone who uses sticks or crutches when out of a wheelchair may find it useful to have clips attached to the chair so that the sticks or crutches are readily available.

Wearing a bulky overcoat to keep warm and dry in a wheelchair may make sitting in the chair a tight squeeze. A coat long enough to sit on may be an impediment when propelling the chair, and the lining may tear with the arm movements. A short cloak or jacket, or a poncho, can be worn instead with a quilted nylon cover, like the bottom half of a sleeping bag, up to the waist. These covers, and also waterproof aprons, are specially designed for wheelchairs. A full length pvc or nylon cloak with a hood is made for use by someone who is being pushed in a chair.

Propelling a wheelchair means usually having dirty hands unless you wear gloves. Leather or leatherette gloves tend to wear out quickly. Gardening gloves are strong enough to stand up to propelling a wheelchair but are not very elegant.

Half-sleeves for wheelchair users, made from plastic material with elastic at the wrists protect cuffs and sleeves from wear and dirt when propelling the chair.

For anyone who cannot look round, a cycle mirror is a useful attachment to the wheelchair. A cycle rear lamp is an extra safety measure if a wheelchair is used outdoors after dark.

Ramps

Where it is necessary to have a ramp built over a flight of steps so that a wheelchair can be used, the local social services department can be asked for help and advice.

—slope and size

A gradient of 1 in 12 is usually the steepest slope for a ramp for a wheelchair user to be able to propel up or a helper to push a chair up easily, provided the ramp is not too long. Where there is space, a ramp with a 1 in 14 gradient is better. Where the space is limited, a ramp of 1 in 10 is possible, and someone with very strong arms might manage a short ramp of 1 in 8.

Where there is not enough room to provide a ramp of a reasonable gradient, a series of steps with treads about 4 feet (about 1·2 metres) deep may solve the problem: a wheelchair can then be pushed up each step as if it were a kerb. A combination of shallow ramps and shallow steps is another possible solution.

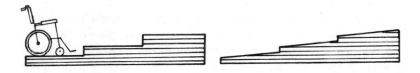

At the top of any ramp approaching a door or gate, a flat area is necessary where the wheelchair can pause to enable the person in the chair to unlock the door without having to try to hold the chair in position on the ramp at the same time. Putting on a wheelchair's brakes while on a ramp is difficult and releasing them is hazardous because of the danger of rolling backwards.

A ramp should not be too narrow. Some allowance must be made for leeway in steering a wheelchair. About 30 inches (about 760 mm) is the minimum; 3 feet (910 mm) is better if there is room. When wheeling a chair up a ramp, it is safer not to go too fast and to concentrate on going up the middle in a straight line. If the chair gets out of control, there is the risk of one wheel coming off the side of the ramp and the chair tipping over. A 2-inch high (50 mm) kerb should be provided on the exposed side of a ramp. A kerb may also be useful on the unexposed side against a wall surface.

A short ramp that climbs only one step is normally safe without handrails. But on a longer ramp, handrails should be provided. A height of about 3 feet (about 910 mm) above the ramp surface is generally suitable but a rail may need to be lower for a wheelchair user.

—surface

The surface of a ramp should be non-slip even when it is wet. Coarse aggregate bitumen, tarmacadam or concrete, or roughened asphalt, would make a suitably textured finish for an outdoor ramp. A herring-bone pattern can be incorporated in concrete to give a non-slip finish. In winter, salt can be put down to melt snow and ice, but where a ramp is very exposed or is likely to be badly affected by frost or snow, a canopy should be put over it.

To cover the whole of an indoor ramp with non-slip material, grooved rubber sheets or tiles are suitable, with the corrugations running at right angles to the line of travel. For a chair that is being pushed, it may be better to have a non-slip area in the middle of the ramp for walking on, for example, non-slip strips stuck at intervals across its middle portion, leaving a smooth surface at the sides for the chair wheels.

movable ramps

It may not be necessary to have a fixed ramp built. The Expamet metal ramp can be bolted on to an existing step and unbolted and moved when necessary. There are indoor and outdoor models. A movable fibreglass reinforced ramp has been designed by the Bath Institute of Medical Engineering and is available from SWIRL, The University, Claverton Down, Bath.

Anyone can get plans for making an inexpensive ramp from wood and angle iron to any required length from the Director of Social Services, County Hall, Chichester, West Sussex.

Lightweight portable ramps are available which can be carried in a wheelchair. These come in pairs so that one wheel goes down each, with a spreader bar to hold them the correct distance apart. They can be used on kerbs or steps up to about 9 inches (230 mm) high. To use these ramps successfully, the wheels and castors of the wheelchair must be in line. To put the ramp down and pick it up as necessary, a wheelchair user must have good trunk and arm muscles.

Hydraulic lifts
Where there is no room to build a ramp of a suitable gradient, it may be possible to install a hydraulic lift alongside front or back door steps if there is a drop of at least 4 feet (1.2 metres).

Hydraulic lifts are rather similar to the lifting platforms that are used outside factories for lifting goods from road level up to floor level. They work on a scissor type of mechanism, which is housed underneath the lifting platform. In order to reach the platform, it is necessary either to have a ramp attached to the edge of the platform or to dig a hole in the ground underneath the lift deep enough to house the mechanism in order to bring the platform down to ground level. Hydraulic lifts are usually designed to go straight up and down, normally up to about 6 feet (about 1.8 metres). A hydraulic lift may also be useful in a split level building where someone needs to be taken up only half a floor so that a rise of about six feet is enough. Hydraulic lifts have safety barriers or gates.

Where there is no room to install an ordinary hydraulic lift alongside a flight of steps, there is the Step-over lift which is designed to be installed at the foot of a flight of steps and to rise up and over the edge of the top step. It requires minimal excavation to accommodate its power unit.

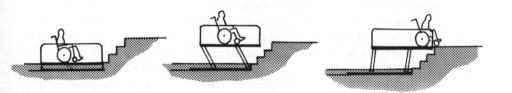

Hoists

Lifting a severely disabled person single-handed is difficult, and can be dangerous both for the person concerned and the helper. A lifting device or a hoist is probably the answer, but it is necessary both to select the most suitable hoist and to train the people concerned in how to use it. The correct technique can make all the manoeuvres easy and comfortable, whereas the wrong slings and inexperienced handling can not only hurt the disabled person but make him fearful for future occasions. The physiotherapist or the occupational therapist at the local hospital or the domiciliary occupational therapist can be asked to advise. Exact measurements of doorways, the layout of the bathroom, and dimensions of other rooms where the hoist may be used, will be needed to check if it can be properly manoeuvred. The local authority may supply a hoist. If you are buying one, ask the manufacturer to demonstrate it in the home beforehand.

There must be adequate space to manoeuvre the hoist and to store it when it is not in use, and a competent person available to operate it and cope with the complexities of the slings if the person concerned cannot manage unaided.

overhead hoists

An overhead hoist can be operated either electrically or manually (working rather like an industrial block and tackle). On a hoist with an electric motor, one string is pulled for raising and lowering, and another for moving sideways. A hoist usually runs on a permanent track, either straight or gently curved. The track has to be fixed through the ceiling to the joists above. It normally has to be bolted through three ceiling joists, not just one. If there is any doubt that the ceiling may not be strong enough to take the weight, a surveyor should be consulted. If the ceiling is structurally unsuitable, a rolled steel joist could be fixed into weight-bearing walls.

It is possible for some people to operate an overhead hoist themselve, without needing a helper.

If the track of an electric hoist is to run into a bathroom or lavatory, a protective isolating transformer should be installed. The installation of an electric hoist must be inspected by the local electricity board.

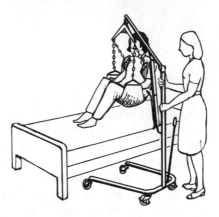

mobile hoists

With a mobile hoist, someone has to be there to help, and work the lifting mechanism. Most mobile hoists are hydraulically operated. Someone who anticipates problems of maintenance may prefer a mechanical system: there is one with a screw mechanism and one with a ratchet and chain mechanism. The lifting mechanism on all hoists requires minimal effort to operate, but pushing a hoist with the person on it can be harder work and some hoists are difficult to wheel.

The smaller hoists are more suitable for use in the home. The hoist must be able to lift the person high enough above the height of the bed or bath rim before being lowered down. It may be possible to lower the height of the bed, but even so, a very small hoist may not lift high enough.

The chassis height of hoists varies and so does the diameter of the wheels. A hoist cannot be used if it cannot be put in position to lift. It works on a cantilever principle, so it must be possible to wheel it into position under a bed, a bath, or perhaps a car. Some beds have very little clearance, and a bath may have to be adapted with part of the side panel cut away to make room for the base of hoist. If there is not

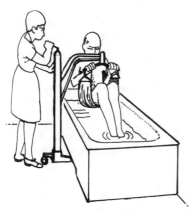

sufficient clearance for it to go underneath, the hoist must be wide enough to fit round a wheelchair, or any other seat that is being used. Several hoists have a chassis that can open out, to straddle a wheelchair, and close, to go through a narrow doorway.

A mobile hoist must be narrow enough, or be designed to be temporarily narrowed enough, to go through the doorways of the rooms where it will be used. It must also be small enough to go round corners—for example, through a doorway into a narrow corridor and then back through the next narrow doorway. One hoist is available with a choice of chassis widths.

A hoist should be stable, but because of the need for movement in a restricted space, there has to be a compromise between manoeuvrability and stability. Some hoists are very stable with the chassis splayed out, but unstable when narrowed to go through doors and down corridors. A swinging movement of the person being carried can cause the hoist to overturn, for instance, when one of the leading castors is wheeled over an obstruction such as a carpet edge and jolts the hoist, or when the person in the hoist leans sideways or swings free of an obstacle. Care should be taken to eliminate or avoid obstructions, and a hoist with an adjustable base should have its chassis widened again as soon as it is through a narrow opening. A hoist with an adjustable base should have stops to prevent the chassis moving in too far for safety, should the narrowing mechanism go wrong.

One small hoist has to be tilted to go over a threshold, those with bigger wheels can ride over such an obstacle. Some hoists have brakes and other do not.

Sometimes it is necessary to put a hoist into the boot of a car. Most mobile hoists take apart. Some just lift to pieces, but with others it is necessary to undo a number of nuts and bolts, which takes much longer. The lengths of the component parts vary, so the size of the car boot into which the hoist is going to be fitted should be checked.

—slings for hoists
There are many different designs of slings. The manufacturer of a hoist should be asked to advise on the various slings that are made for use with his hoist.

The method of slinging must be safe so that there is no danger of the person falling out. It must be comfortable: some people can tolerate being lifted on narrow slings, others need a much wider area of sling to spread the load. The slings must be easy to use. Putting on slings can be very difficult at first, and it may take a long time and a lot of perseverance to get used to them. Choosing the most appropriate method of slinging needs care and skill. Doctors and therapists in hospitals and special centres who are used to dealing with hoists can advise on both the choice of hoist and sling and the best technique to use. The Disabled Living Foundation in London has many hoists on display, and these can be tried out, by appointment.

There are two main slinging methods, one using two slings, the other a hammock type support. With the two-sling method, which is generally the easiest method when the person is lying on the bed, narrow straps are easier to put on, wider ones are more comfortable. Adjusting the chains which hold the slings alters the angle at which the person is carried: a different position may give more stability. Someone with severe loss of muscle power may tend to jack-knife and slip between two slings, and may therefore be safer in a hammock type sling.

A hammock type of sling is better for someone who finds two slings either uncomfortable or unsafe. It is also better for someone who goes into spasm or who has painful joints. In a hammock sling, joint movement is minimised. Some hammock slings are split at one end to provide individual leg slings. This is probably the easiest type of sling to put on someone in a wheelchair. Some hammock slings have a commode aperture and others provide head support.

If a sling needs adapting for a particular use, you should ask the manufacturer to make the appropriate adjustments or to provide a specially designed sling. It is his responsibility to see that the special sling is safe for the use to which it will be put.

The slings which hold the person in position are attached by chains to a spreader bar which is hooked on to the lifting arm of the hoist. Spreader bars come in several sizes and it is important to choose the right size. If the bar is too narrow, the slings will grip and chafe the body. If it is too wide, the slings will be too loose and the person may slip. The right size is usually the narrowest bar that gives support without chafing.

A coathanger-shaped bar swings the person less than a straight bar. The Mecalift hoist has a rigid cross bar and very short chains to its slings and therefore swings very little.

The chains which attach the slings to the spreader bar must be carefully adjusted because they determine the angle at which the person is carried. This adjustment is done by moving the chains up or down a link on the spreader bar hooks which hold them. It is usually best to hoist someone in the position in which he feels most comfortable and secure, but when being hoisted into a car, it may be necessary to be carried in a semi-lying position using the shortest possible amount of chain in order to manoeuvre through the small space between the roof of the car and the car seat.

other lifting devices

There are lifting devices which are entirely rigid, the seat being an integral part of the hoist and not suspended from it, therefore it does not swing. One which works on this priciple is the Ambulift, which has a lavatory type seat attached direct to the pillar of the hoist. It can have a leg rest extension which slides into the front of the seat to lift someone with legs outstretched and then lower him—for instance, into the bath. This type of device is not suitable for a severely paralysed person: sitting on the seat requires more muscle power than being lifted on slings.

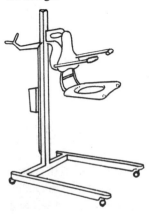

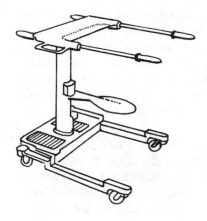

The Arjo Pilot has a flat spade-shaped seat which is mounted on a pillar, and can be raised and lowered. The seat can project forward to put someone on a bed or into a walk-in bath and can be pulled out from beneath him after he has sat down. The whole device wheels like a walking trolley, and can even be used as a walking aid. It is not suitable for someone with very weak muscles.

maintenance

A hoist or lifting device should be checked when delivered, and maintained regularly thereafter. An annual inspection is usually sufficient, but the manufacturer should be asked to give guidance on this. It is wise to check the materials, stitching and fastenings; the seals of a hydraulic system; the general condition of chains, wires or cords; the tightness of nuts and bolts, lock nuts or washers at critical points.

Anyone who has difficulty or feels unsafe in the bath should avoid bathing when alone in the house. Someone who lives alone should arrange for a friend or relative to come round to be there, just in case, while having a bath. A telephone, on a long lead, taken into the bathroom is another precaution. It is unwise to lock the bathroom door. If you want to be able to lock the door, fit the type of lock which, in an emergency, can be unlocked from the outside with a coin or a screwdriver.

Someone who lives alone and can manage to bath unaided but is afraid of getting stuck in the bath or falling, and has no one who can come to the house, might consider using the public baths. These are usually kept very clean, the hot water costs less than at home, and there is an attendant who would come to the rescue if anything happened.

To get help with bathing at home, your general practitioner should be asked to contact the area health authority. The local social services department could also be asked about getting someone to help you bath. In some areas, bathing attendants are employed whose job is to give baths to people who are unable to bath themselves. Bath attendants are not nurses, and do not carry out nursing duties. An attendant will usually come regularly once, or perhaps twice, a week. A patient unable to leave the bed, or who needs to use a hoist to get into and out of the bath, will probably be visited by a district nursing sister. Male nurses or bath attendants are sometimes available for men.

Aids such as a bath seat or a rail can be supplied by the social services department; an occupational therapist should advise on the most suitable aids, and how to use them.

The bathroom
The bathroom floor should be covered with a non-slip surface, such as sealed cork or unpolished vinyl, and kept in good condition. Never polish the bathroom floor. A mop for wiping up spilled water should be kept handy. A large, absorbent, non-slip bath mat on the floor will both soak up splashed water and help to dry the feet. A thick, looped cotton mat with non-slip underlay is good.

If you are slow in getting out of the bath, and in drying and dressing, you may get cold, so the bathroom should be heated. A central heating radiator or a radiant wall heater fixed high up would be suitable. A low powered tubular heater at skirting board level, covered with a guard, can be left on all the time and is economical to run. A heated towel rail provides some background heating (but should not be used as a grab rail because it may not be firmly enough fixed, and will be hot). A portable electric fire must never be taken into the bathroom.

The basin, the taps and any other fittings should not be used for support, because these are not built to take body weight. Suitable rails should be provided instead.

When the light switch is a cord swinging from the ceiling, it may be difficult to grasp especially when holding on to a walking stick or frame, and difficult to find in the dark. The cord could be threaded through a screw eye to hold it in a convenient position, and have a large knob or ring at the end to grasp. A conventional wall switch outside the door may be a better alternative.

The bath
If a new bath is needed—for example, when creating a downstairs bathroom for a disabled or elderly person—choose one that will be most suitable for the person who is going to use it.

Baths are described according to their outside length; the length at the waterline is always less. A short bath—say, a 5-foot (about 1·5 metres) bath—is quite adequate and feels comfortably safe because it would be impossible to slide right under the water. It is also more economical on bath water. A short bath is not suitable when an inside bath seat is needed to help you get on to the bottom of the bath because there will not be enough room for both you and the seat.

Lower than usual baths—say, 16 inches (about 400 mm) high—are available, and also baths with a lower section in the middle of one side. A low bath is easiest for someone who steps into the bath, and also for someone who gets into the bath by sitting on a stool beside the bath and then lifting or swinging the feet over the rim of the bath. Someone getting into a bath from a wheelchair needs a bath the same height as the chair—that is, about 19 inches (about 480 mm) high.

The depth inside the bath should also be considered. A shallow bath is easier to step into and out of and is also easier for getting a good leverage on the rim to get up from the bottom of the bath.

Some baths are flat on the bottom. This makes it safer to stand on. A few baths are now made with a non-slip area on part of the bottom.

A bath with hand grips built into both sides provides handholds for someone who lacks confidence or is generally rather weak. But they are less useful for someone who cannot bend at the hips.

If a portable hoist is to be used, there must be a sufficient clearance under the bath. The side panels may have to be removed or a recess cut in the bottom of the panel. A recess along the bottom of the panel or setting the bath panel at an angle enables a helper to get her feet closer to the bath and so lessens back strain when helping to lift. This also gives more space for manoeuvring a wheelchair (having swinging or detachable foot rests on the chair also helps).

Cutting a recess into the top of the side panel can produce a useful hand hold. A hardwood fillet fixed along the length of the bath under the bath rim provides a comfortable grip.

A walk-in bath has a side-hinged or removable door and a built-in seat opposite the door. Once the door is shut, the water is run into the bath from a mixer tap (a thermostatically controlled mixer tap can be fitted but at a considerable additional cost). Afterwards the bather has to pull out the plug, and wait for the bath to empty before he can open the door and get out. It is therefore especially important to have the bathroom warm. This bath is not suitable for someone who cannot sit with knees and hips at right angles, and who cannot walk in, or transfer into it from a wheelchair. A walk-in bath is expensive, and the bather may still need some help, but it does save a helper from any lifting.

non-slip mats

Everyone who has any difficulty with bathing should have some form of a non-slip safeguard in the bottom of the bath, especially with a shiny, new bath.

The most usual method is to have a non-slip mat inside the bath. A rubber mat with a non-slip surface and multiple small suction cups on the underside which adhere to the bath is safer than the type of mat with a few large suction cups which button on to the mat, because they may come unbuttoned. A non-slip mat works most effectively if the bottom of the bath is wet. The mat must be pushed down firmly to make the suckers work. Mats should be cleaned regularly because soap in the bath water can make them slippery.

The mat must be positioned so that it comes under your feet when you stand up in the bath. Usually this means putting the edge of the mat to the edge of the plughole. Mats come in different lengths. Some people prefer to sit on the mat, others just to put their feet on it.

Non-slip mats are available quite cheaply from many chemists. Local social services departments supply them, but it may be quicker and easier to buy one from a shop.

Another method is to attach non-slip strips permanently to the bottom of the bath. These are usually $\frac{3}{4}$ in (20 mm) wide and are self-adhesive. They can be bought either in strips or on a roll from large chemists and hardware stores. Strips may be safer for a very heavy person whose movements could dislodge a bath mat. It is also possible to buy the adhesive material in decorative shapes including flowers, in various colours. These are available in haberdashery departments, usually in the gadget section. If the bath is also used for soaking and drip-drying clothes, frequent contact with detergent may unstick these strips or shapes.

When a bath has a built-in non-slip area, this does not necessarily eliminate the need for a non-slip bath mat or non-slip strips.

filling the bath
Filling the bath before getting in makes it easier to get the right temperature without the danger of running hot water and manipulating taps while sitting in the bath. Also, the buoyancy of the water helps lower the body gently to the bottom.

The Plug-o-matic is a device for controlling the level of the bath water. It is a balloon attached at an adjustable distance from the plug. The balloon floats on the surface of the water. If the water level rises above the chosen depth, the balloon pulls out the plug. This can be a useful precaution for an absent-minded or slow-moving person.

taps

Control of the taps may be a problem where reaching to the far end of the bath is difficult. Taps in the midway position are easier. Thermostatically controlled taps eliminate the risk of scalding but are expensive.

Taps which have a wide cross at the top provide better leverage and are easier to turn than modern streamlined taps. Soft washers can be fitted to some types of tap so that the tap turns off with only gentle pressure.

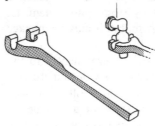

Tap turners with long handles can be made or bought. The extra length of handle makes turning the tap easy. Sometimes a turner can be left wedged on the tap; otherwise, it has to be placed in position each time it is used.

A lever as an integral part of the tap is the easiest to manage but taps with long levers are not normally permitted by water authorities for domestic use. The Levatap has a short lever arm and can be fitted in place of the head of a conventional tap.

bath rails

Most methods of getting down into the bath, and getting up again, are more effective, and in some cases will only be possible, if suitable bath rails are provided. But placing the feet correctly before moving, and timing the thrust which is needed from the feet at a particular moment, is every bit as important as the help given by a rail, especially if your arms are not strong.

Rails, hand grips and poles must be very securely fixed by someone skilled at the job who knows whether the structure of walls, ceiling and other anchor points can take the strain. They must be capable of being abused: a bather may rest almost the whole weight of his body on a rail or may put a pulling strain on just one end of it.

It may be possible to buy a ready-made rail the size and length required, or it may be necessary to buy a piece of tubing or wood the right length and fix it to the wall with flanged brackets. The surface finish of the rail is important because it may be gripped with a wet hand. With a vertical rail, or a diagonal rail, it is especially important to have a non-slip surface. One of the most effective ways is to wind self-adhesive non-slip tape in a spiral round the rail or pole. A plain unvarnished wooden rail is non-slip.

A bath rail must be of sufficient diameter to be comfortably gripped —not less than $1\frac{1}{4}$ inches (about 30 mm). It must have sufficient wall clearance not to scrape the knuckles. With a straight or sloping rail, it must be possible to press down with the forearm on both the rail and the adjoining wall at the same time. A clearance of about two inches will probably be needed.

The right position for a rail depends on your method of getting in and out of the bath. A horizontal rail at hip height is a good general purpose rail. It will help someone whose main disability is lack of confidence. It can be held with either one hand or both, while stepping in or out, when sitting down or getting up, and to steady oneself while washing.

The type of handrail which attaches to the taps and rests on the sides of the bath is more easily fitted than any other. Some models hook only over the taps and are unstable; others clamp on. A rail held on the taps is functionally too low to be really useful but can help to give confidence when stepping into or out of the bath. Nor is it in the most useful position for getting up from the bottom of the bath because only a strong person could pull himself up by it.

It is important that somebody knowledgeable assesses where the rail should be put. If it is as little as two inches wrong, it may be useless. If you want the social services department to put in a rail for you, you have to be prepared for delays while estimates for the work are being obtained and the job done.

getting into the bath from standing
It is safer for someone who is unsteady when standing on one leg to get into the bath from the sitting position. But if someone insists on stepping into the bath, it is best to provide aids to make this safer. A pole could be put between the floor and the ceiling, 15 inches to 18 inches (380 mm to 460 mm) from the tap end of the access side of the bath, to act as a pivot, allowing the body to turn through 90° when stepping into or out of the bath. The pole should be about $1\frac{1}{2}$ inches (40 mm) in diameter. It can be reached from a sitting position inside the bath so is also a help when rising and when reaching forward to turn the taps. But it requires a strong grip on the part of the user. A vertical pole must be attached very securely to a ceiling joist or a bridge between joists. Wet hands slip too easily on a smooth pole, so it should be made of unsealed wood which absorbs water or be covered in non-slip material.

A handrail which clamps to the side of the bath is another aid for stepping into the bath. This should normally be positioned at the tap end of the bath so as to allow maximum room for lifting the legs in. One type is screwed to the floor and clamped between the bath panel and the inside of the bath. It is adjustable in height. Another has clamps but does not reach the floor and therefore is not quite so stable. If attaching such a rail to a fibreglass bath, it may be necessary to insert a block of wood between the side of the bath and the bath panel to prevent the metal hooks penetrating the wall of the bath, but the advice of the manufacturer of the bath should be sought first.

A vertical rail on the wall alongside the bath can be used as well as or instead of a horizontal handrail. The choice depends on whether you are better at pushing or pulling: you pull on a vertical rail and push up on a horizontal rail.

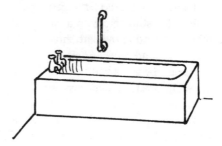

getting into the bath from sitting

For anyone who has difficulty with getting into a bath, it is easier and safer to do so from the sitting position. Some people manage by sitting on the rim of the bath at the corner where it is wider. With some baths, there is a tiled or formica section level with the bath rim at the far end of the bath which can be used as a seat. If the tiles are cold to sit on they can be covered with a cork mat or a towel.

A kitchen stool with a generous sized top of, say, 14 inches (355 mm) square, makes a good seat. The legs should be spaced wide enough to be stable but not so splayed out at the base as to prevent the stool fitting close up against the bath. The stool should be at least as high as the bath. Someone with stiff hips will find a slightly higher stool easier.

Sitting on the stool, lift the legs over the side and into the bath, leaning back a bit if necessary as you do so. (If you have difficulty in getting a weak leg into the bath, lifting it with the hand under the thigh may help.) You then have to lower yourself down the bath. Lean forward and transfer your weight to your feet, using a handgrip for support. From this semi-standing position, lower yourself to the bottom of the bath.

—after a stroke

If you have had a stroke, you may feel safer putting the good leg into the bath first, and so being able to use the good arm to hold on to a rail on the wall. This may mean getting into the bath with your back to the taps. You can protect yourself from the taps by binding several thicknesses of towel round them.

There is a method for getting down into, and up from, the bath mainly for someone with a paralysed arm and leg (but also useful for others). Stand in the bath, hold on to a horizontal rail on the wall with the good hand, kneel down on the affected knee and then on the good knee, put the good hand on the bottom of the bath so that you are in the crawling position, and turn over towards the affected side until sitting down in the bath.

To get up, lift the affected leg over the other, or put the good leg underneath it. Twist away from the affected side and put the good hand on the bottom of the bath. Push on the hand and the knee of the good leg, and turn over into the crawling position. Raise your head and grasp the handrail. Bring the good leg forward and stand up on it, pressing the shoulder against the wall at the side of the bath for extra support. This method is not suitable when the bath is especially narrow or the bather is especially broad.

Although complicated to describe, many people prefer this method to the alternative of cluttering up the bath with seats. It helps to practise the manoeuvre on the floor first. It is also a useful way of getting up from the floor after a fall.

bath boards

Someone who has difficulty in taking weight on the feet, may find a board across the bath helpful. You may be able to lower yourself from the bath board on to an inside bath seat and from this to the bottom of the bath; or you may prefer to remain sitting on the bath board and wash from a basin placed on a board or a stool in the bath.

A bath board is not very suitable for someone with stiff hips who needs to lean well back in the bath, because it will get in the way unless someone is there to remove it. Someone in a wheelchair can transfer from the chair by sliding on to a bath board, lifting the legs into the bath before or after moving on to the board. If the bath is too high, try an extra seat cushion on the chair to help equalise the heights.

A bath board can be bought or made, but it must be the right size for the bath and constructed so that it cannot slip or tip in use. The board should fit as near to the end of the bath as possible and close to the wall alongside. On a home-made board, wooden blocks should be put underneath to fit closely to the contour of the inside of the bath. The nearside corner should be rounded to prevent it digging into the thigh. The board can be covered with cork, which will feel warm, or in plastic sheeting for someone who needs to slide along it.

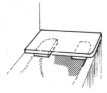

A bath board can be linked to a stool beside the bath by two metal hooks and sockets. This is easier to get on to than just a board and provides a hand support while you move across over the bath. The stool and board must be very firmly held together for safety. The stool on its own may also be useful at the washbasin, and can be moved out of the room when not in use.

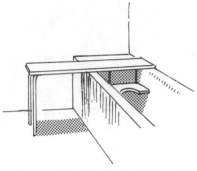

A combined bath stool, board and seat can be bought. In a small bathroom this takes up a lot of permanent space.

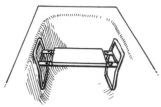

bath seats

Inside bath seats are designed to help people to get down into the bath or up from the bottom, when they cannot get down or up in one movement. Once you are sitting on the bottom of the bath, the seat can be taken out, to make more room while actually washing. If you cannot reach the bottom of the bath, you can wash sitting on the seat.

There is a wide variety of bath seats on the market. Some wedge into the bath, some hook over the edge and some stand on the bottom of the bath. Some are attached to a combined bath board and stool. When a bath seat is used without a bath board, it can go farther back in the bath, depending on the curve of the bath, and so be less in the way.

A bath seat must be strong and stable because the bather may press down on one corner when getting up out of the bath. A seat that wedges into the bath is usually the most stable type.

A fibreglass bath may not be strong enough to take the pressure from a wedge-in bath seat or one standing on legs. With a fibreglass bath, it is better to use a seat which hooks over the sides of the bath, even though this can be more easily knocked out of position.

Bath seats which stand on legs in the bath are available in the form of a lavatory seat with the front cut out, like a horseshoe, for easier washing. But a wedge-in seat provides a wider area for sitting down safely, and most people can tilt sideways sufficiently on one to wash between their legs.

It is more difficult to get from the bottom of the bath onto the seat, than from the seat to the rim. If the seat is to be used to help someone get to the bottom of the bath and up again, it should be positioned somewhat less than halfway up from the bottom of the bath to make it easier to get on to. When used just as a seat, it should be a little above the halfway mark. Baths vary in size so it may be necessary to buy an adjustable seat or to make one to fit the individual bath. The seat should be placed firmly in position in the bath before the water is run in.

—using bath boards and bath seats

Sitting on a bath stool or on a bath board or its extension, after lifting or swinging the legs into the bath you have to move across onto the centre of the bath board. Pushing down on the board with one hand while pulling on a rail on the wall with the other hand is a good way of shifting the weight sideways. But it is important that you push both upwards and sideways, otherwise you just raise yourself up from the seat and sit down again in the same position.

Getting down on the inside bath seat entails leaning forward and pressing down on the hands or forearms to take the weight off the hips. By pushing the body forward and at the same time gradually letting go of this downward push, the hips can be lowered to the seat below. There are different ways of taking the pressure on the hands or forearms. Some people can press down with both hands on the board at the side of the hips. Others take the weight on the forearm on the free side of the bath, leaning well over as they do so and pressing down on the bath board with the other hand.

The RICA report on bath aids (No 13, December 1972) shows how a diagonal bath rail which slopes downwards and forwards can be used in conjunction with a bath board and seat, to make getting down into

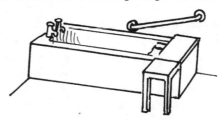

the bath easier by leaning on the rail as you lower yourself into the bath. This rail follows the line of movement. It must have a non-slip surface to make it easy to grasp firmly.

Someone who uses a bath seat without a bath board because his only difficulty is getting down to and up from the bottom of the bath, may want a rail within easy reach all the way. A hand rail which slopes downwards and backwards to finish just in front of the seat allows the hand to move along the rail both while sitting down gently on the seat and when pulling forward and up from it. The other hand can grip the bath rim.

bath shells

If you have difficulty in getting out of the bath tub because it is too deep, a bath shell may be helpful. This is a moulded shape which fits over the existing bath to convert it to a shallower bath. One model has a flat base, another provides support in a half-sitting position. Both types enable a person to get in and out of the bath more easily from a sitting position. The bath shell fills from the normal bath taps and empties into the bath.

lifting cushion

Another aid for getting down into the bath is the Tamplin lifting bath cushion. The cushion is put into the bath, connected to the tap and filled with water until the top of the cushion is level with the rim of the bath. You then get on to it at this level and let the water run out of it into the bath. The cushion with you on it sinks gently to the bottom. To get up again, the cushion is filled up with water from the taps to lift you up in the bath. This cushion may feel unsteady and filling and emptying is not easy to operate. so a helper should be at hand if it is used.

getting out of the bath

Getting out of the bath is more difficult than getting in, but the buoyancy of the water helps. If you are afraid of falling and slipping under the water, the plug can be pulled out first so that the water is in the process of running away. (If it is difficult to reach the plug, the chain can be hooked with a walking stick.)

The action of getting out of the bath is the reverse of getting in. It is important to tuck the feet back as far as possible to bring the body's centre of gravity forward. If there is a bath board, the action of getting up involves pushing upwards and then backwards, in order to clear the edge of the board. If there is no bath board in the way and you are going to sit on a platform at the end of the bath or the corner of the bath rim, pushing up backwards is sufficient. With a forward-sloping diagonal rail, you press on the rail with one hand and on the rim of the bath with the other and push with the feet.

If you take the weight of your body on one forearm by leaning on the free side of the bath when getting out, a damp towel or a flannel placed along the rim of the bath provides a useful non-slip surface to hold on to.

When another person is giving assistance, she should face the opposite way to the bather and stand, feet apart, with one foot in front of the other and the knees slightly bent. Hooking her arm under the bather's from the front and pushing with her other hand on the bath rim, she can help him to rise by straightening her knees and hips; she should at the same time keep her back flat.

bath hoists

A general purpose hoist can be used in the bathroom. Some mobile hoists can be lifted off their chassis into a floor fixture or can be bought without their chassis to be fixed permanently to the floor.

There are specially designed bath hoists which have a seat shaped like a lavatory seat, attached to a vertical bar. This seat can be raised and lowered by turning a handle at the top of the vertical bar. You start by sitting on the seat outside the bath, with your back to the taps. You

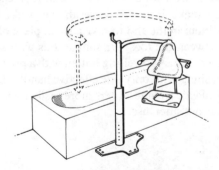

wind the handle to raise the seat above the rim of the bath, then swivel round over the bath, lifting your feet in and turning until you are facing the taps. You then wind yourself down into the bath. Getting out is the reverse action. This method can be managed safely without help provided you are able to push on the bathroom walls or to push or pull on some other support outside the bath in order to swivel the hoist round. You must also be able to lift your legs over the edge of the bath. One type of bath hoist (the Solo-Bath) clamps over the edge of the bath, the other (the Autolift) is screwed to the floor beside the bath.

Washing

A shower unit fitted to the bath taps may be useful, especially for someone who has to sit on a bath seat and has difficulty with washing the top part of the body. A cheap rubber version can be bought from any chemist, and a more expensive flexible metal type from a plumber. It may be advisable to have a plastic curtain to draw round part or all of the bath, keeping it inside the bath, to avoid flooding the bathroom floor.

A soap rack across the bath may be a hazard when getting in and out of the bath; one that hooks over the side may be less in the way. A soap niche in the tiles above the bath is even better. An oval of rubber with suckers all over both sides, called an octopus, available in many chemists and hardware stores, sticks both to the wall and to the soap. Soap with a hole in the middle and a loop of cord through it to be hung around the neck is made for showers but can be used in the bath, too.

Long-handled bath brushes, long-handled sponges and loofahs, available from most big chemists, can be used for reaching the back, legs and feet. A dish mop with a foam rubber head or one made from soft strips of material can be useful for washing the back of the neck and the ears. A loofah with wide tape sewn on to each end with loops for the hands may make it easier to scrub the back. A length of dowelling with a slit cut in the end to take a small piece of sponge can be used to wash between the toes. Or similar aids with sponges on a long handle can be bought. A towelling mitten with a pocket that takes soap is good for washing with only one effective hand or if your hands are stiff or weak. A plastic sponge lathers more easily than a flannel and is easier to squeeze out after use.

For someone who is unable to take a bath, sitting or perching on a stool or chair is a safe position for an all-over wash. A folded towel on the seat may help. The floor should be covered with a sizeable plastic sheet or an extra large bath mat. A plastic bowl on the floor filled from a plastic jug, or a plastic bucket lowered to the floor with the water already in it can be used for washing legs and feet. A good soak may ease the feet. The lower part of the body should be washed first and dried, and then the upper part washed from the wash basin.

Drying
After a bath or a strip wash, it is generally easiest to dry with a very large towel or a bath sheet which can be wrapped round the body to absorb the dampness without the effort of rubbing dry. If there is a bathroom chair with a back, the towel can be draped over the back of the chair ready to be sat on. But for someone with weak arms or painful hands, a small light towel is easier to manage. A towelling cape which can be bought in the beachwear department of a big store, or a large dressing-gown made of towelling, may also be useful.

Having a loop on the towel so that it can be hooked to the wall may help someone to dry with only one useful hand.

Cleaning the bath
It is easier to clean the bath when it is still warm (and you may manage to clean it while you are still in it). Kneeling beside the bath is a good position from which to exert pressure and rub the bath, and the bath itself provides firm support for getting down and up. Alternatively, the bath can be cleaned while sitting alongside on a chair; using a sponge or mop with an extended handle will minimise bending.

Showers
The alternative to a bath may be a shower. A shower takes up less space in the room and for some people may be easier to use. A shower cabinet need not necessarily be in the bathroom: one can be put in a downstairs cloakroom, a bedroom or any other room. The siting of a shower may depend on the plumbing and the water pressure available;

this should be checked with a plumber beforehand. A report on showers in *Handyman Which?* November 1974 dealt with types and brands, plumbing and installation.

Most shower cabinets have a 6-inch to 9-inch threshold (about 150 mm to 230 mm), both to contain the water and to house the drain. (It may be possible to do without this barrier and have a sloping floor to the outlet drain.) The floor should be made of non-slip material, or strips of non-slip material should be fitted to the floor.

A vertical grab rail at the entrance to the shower is advisable. Horizontal rails fixed to the side walls may help to give confidence and maintain balance.

A seat in the shower may be an advantage. A wooden bench could be fixed to the wall at a suitable height, with a horizontal rail on the adjacent wall about 10 inches (about 250 mm) above the level of the seat to help in getting up and to hold on to while washing. It is possible to buy a shower seat, shaped like a lavatory seat with the front cut away for ease of washing, set on four legs (or a wooden kitchen chair or a plastic chair with rubber ferrules on the legs could be used). A more stable alternative is a shower seat on a two-legged frame designed to wedge diagonally across a standard built-in shower unit. In a shower without a threshold, a chair with wheels could be used for getting into the shower. The Chiltern shower unit has been designed for easy access and use in a wheeled shower chair. Some commodes on wheels are suitable for use in a shower.

A wheelchair user, to transfer sideways, needs a bench on a side wall of the shower cabinet, and a rail on the back wall.

It is important to be able to reach the taps easily, especially when sitting on a seat. A thermostatically controlled shower tap unit is safer than having to adjust the water temperature yourself.

The type of shower head on a flexible hose can be taken off the wall to use as a hand-held spray or hooked on the wall at various levels—for instance, shoulder, hip and leg height—leaving both hands free for washing or holding on to a grab rail. There is a shower head which slides up or down the wall on a track, but this may need a strong hand to adjust.

It is possible to dry immediately inside the shower cabinet. A large towel or towelling robe should be within easy reach just outside the cabinet. The room should be heated.

Cleaning the teeth

The handle of a toothbrush can be enlarged or lengthened in the same way as the handle of any other implement. Another way of making it easier to hold a toothbrush is to fit a wide elastic band round the palm of the hand with a loop in it to hold the toothbrush handle. It does not matter if the elastic gets wet when the teeth are brushed.

Some people find an electric toothbrush easier to use than a manually operated brush. The handle is bigger and easier to hold and less wrist and arm movement is required.

A metal or plastic key for helping to squeeze toothpaste out of the tube is available.

Shaving

A safety razor handle can be made thicker by any of the methods described for knives and forks.

An electric razor is usually more convenient to use than a safety razor. It is easier to grip and requires less precision. A *Which?* report on shaving was published in December 1975 and on battery shavers in September 1973.

A wall-mounted razor holder has been designed to enable someone to shave by moving his head against the razor. The holder is not being manufactured but construction drawings are available free from Braun Electric, Staines.

Someone in a wheelchair or who needs to shave sitting down may be unable to see properly in the existing bathroom mirror. A tall looking-glass on the wall of the bathroom can be put at a suitable height both for sitting and for standing.

Finger nails

Someone with a weak grip may find a nailbrush with a curved handle that fits round the hand is satisfactory. For someone who can use only one hand when washing, a nailbrush can be attached with suction cups to a smooth surface, such as the side of a basin. Two suction cups could be screwed into the back of a wooden nailbrush, or any nailbrush with a flat enough back can be attached to an octopus soap holder. When a nailbrush is fixed in position, the hand can be moved across the brush rather than the other way round.

It is better to file the finger nails frequently, instead of cutting them. If you are unable to hold the file steady, mount it in a wooden tool handle and hold it between the knees, or jam a long file in a drawer.

The hair

For someone with stiff shoulders and elbows who finds it difficult to comb the hair, there is a simple way of making a long-handled comb. Take about 10 inches (250 mm) of broom handle and drill holes through it to take a tail comb. Having several holes means you can move the comb to various convenient angles.

When washing the hair over a washbasin, a plastic hose attached to the taps will make the job easier. If you find it difficult to bend forward sufficiently, there are basins on stands designed for washing the hair backwards and portable plastic bowls for washing the hair of a person lying in bed.

A local hairdresser may be prepared to come to the home, especially mid-week when not so busy. Pensioners who can get out of the house may find that they can have their hair done more cheaply at a hairdresser's on certain days of the week. For someone in a wheelchair, it may not be possible to use the backwash basin or hood drier, so enquire about facilities before going to the hairdresser's.

The lavatory is the place where everybody would wish to be independent. To be forced to accept help, however kindly given, can be demoralising.

Many disabled people need more space for manoeuvring than other people, and the lavatory is usually the smallest room in the house. Rehanging the door to open outwards not only provides more space but makes a rescue operation easier should someone collapse inside. It is safest not to lock the door, but if this possible infringement of privacy is unacceptable, a lock which in an emergency can be opened from outside with a coin or a screwdriver should be fitted.

Where the lavatory is next to the bathroom, there may be advantages in knocking down the wall between them. This provides more space for manoeuvre in both rooms and makes washing the hands after using the lavatory easier. But in a busy household, where other people want to use either, it means a longer wait and this can be embarrassing.

In some houses, it is necessary to climb up a steep flight of stairs to get to the lavatory or, much worse, go out of doors in all weathers. Getting to the lavatory can be made safer by the installation of more adequate lighting with conveniently positioned switches, and by providing handrails on steps or stairs. If the lavatory is outside, building a covered way and smoothing an uneven path will help. For a wheelchair user, it may be possible to provide a ramp.

The lavatory should be heated, especially if it is an outdoor one. A low-powered tubular heater at skirting board level is economic to run and can be safely left on all the time. It should be covered with a guard. A heater at this level is more effective than an overhead radiant heater because it is the unclothed, lower part of the body which needs warming. It is possible to buy a lavatory seat with an electrically heated cover, but it is usually better to heat the room rather than just the seat. There are also cushioned lavatory seats of plastic foam, upholstered with pvc.

When installing a new lavatory, the position of the cistern should be considered. A high cistern leaves more room for someone with stiff hips who needs to lean backwards, and for someone with a backward curvature of the spine. A low level cistern can be useful to lean against for support; with a modern slimline version, it is possible to lean back farther, which would be useful for someone with stiff hips. A foot-controlled flush can be installed for someone who has very weak arms.

Putting in a lavatory for a disabled person because there is no accessible lavatory in the house may qualify for a local authority grant. The layout of the house determines where a downstairs lavatory can be added. The Building Regulations stipulate that a lavatory must not be built directly off a kitchen without a lobby in between.

Getting on and off the seat

Getting down to and up from a lavatory seat is similar to the action of getting into and out of a chair, with the additional complication of having to manage clothes. Because of this someone who needs no help with getting up from a chair may need help in the lavatory. If you find a higher chair easier to get up from, you may need a raised lavatory seat, and someone who finds it necessary to pull up on the arms of a chair or on some nearby piece of furniture may need a grab rail in the lavatory. A kitchen stool placed near the lavatory may help by providing something firm to lean on when sitting down and getting up.

Someone with very stiff hips or knees or who wears calipers may find that the feet slide forward on the floor when trying to get up. This problem can be solved by nailing a small strip of wood across the floor to act as a foot stop, or by sticking non-slip strips to the floor to give better foot purchase. Inflated or padded seats are available which are more comfortable when wearing a ring caliper.

raised lavatory seats

Most lavatories vary in height between 14 and 16 inches (approximately 350 mm to 410 mm). A low seat is generally easier for a frail elderly person. Someone with painful or stiff joints or very weak legs will find a higher seat—say, up to 20 inches (about 500 mm)—easier for getting on and off.

For a seat to be permanently raised, it is best to have the whole lavatory pan higher. This is more expensive than having a removable raised seat but is less conspicuous. It is possible to buy a lavatory unit with a high pedestal. Another firm makes a fireclay base 3 inches (about 75 mm) high to be installed under a lavatory pedestal, or a shaped wooden block can be used. Because it is easier to defaecate in a squatting position, a footstool should be used.

A number of removable raised lavatory seats are available which sit directly in the lavatory pan. (They are unstable if placed on the lavatory seat.) The lightness of the seat and whether it fits easily on to the pan is important if a disabled person has to lift it on and off. Some seats come in different heights, some are adjustable in height and some also adjust to fit different sizes of lavatory pan. Some have a metal or plastic lining inside the raised part which makes cleaning easier. Some are higher at the back than at the front and this makes a more comfortable seat for someone with a stiff hip. Travelling with a raised lavatory seat can be an embarrassment. One possible solution is to take a clean motor scooter tyre which can be put on top of a lavatory seat.

Seats are available made of lightweight moulded plastic, 4 to 6 inches (100 to 150 mm) high, with a slightly concave rim which gives a feeling of security. They either clip on to a standard lavatory pan or fit into the pan with non-slip pads on the underside to make it even more stable. Being moulded in one piece, these seats are easy to keep clean. Seats made with a convex rim are less comfortable; also, a thin person may tend to slide towards the middle.

A home-made method is to build a hinged flap with a hole in it at the desired height over the lavatory. This has the advantage of providing support for the hands on either side when getting down and up.

handrails

If an adjacent washbasin is the most convenient grabbing point, it must be strengthened with supports under the front and down to the floor to make it safe. Other favourite grabbing points are the lavatory paper fitting, a towel rail and, in a small room, the door knob. None of these can be made safe, and something stronger should be used instead. For example, to avoid holding on to a door fitting, especially if the door opens inwards, a D-handle could be attached to the frame of the door.

Any grab rail, wherever it is fitted, must be firmly enough attached to be able to take the strain of the body's weight in any direction. Some walls, by their construction, are not strong enough to take this strain; sometimes a floor fixing as well as a wall fixing is needed. Long thick screws must be used; the screw holes in the brackets may need to be enlarged to take thick enough screws.

A horizontal rail at waist level can be a useful multi-purpose rail. It is helpful when walking into the room, when manipulating clothing, when a man is standing at the lavatory, and when sitting down and getting up.

A lower horizontal rail makes a useful aid to push up on in a similar way to the arm of a chair. It can be fixed to the wall if this is near enough to the pedestal.

In some cases, a horizontal rail is needed on both sides of the lavatory, just at the pedestal or going all the way to the door. This enables you to hold one rail when facing the lavatory and the other when facing away from it. Someone who normally uses a wheelchair may be able to walk into the lavatory with the support of two rails if the room is narrow enough.

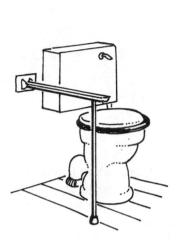

As an alternative, a hinged rail can be bought which fixes to the back wall and can be folded up against the wall out of the way when not required. Two of these may be needed, one on each side of the lavatory.

A vertical rail is useful for someone with stiff hips who cannot lean forward and press down on a horizontal rail and therefore needs to pull on a rail in front. It is also useful for someone with limited reach because it provides a choice of heights.

A diagonal rail is a useful multi-purpose rail. It conforms to the pattern of movement of standing and sitting, and therefore the hand can move along it throughout the movement, giving a feeling of stability. But gripping at this angle can be awkward and painful for someone with arthritic wrists and hands.

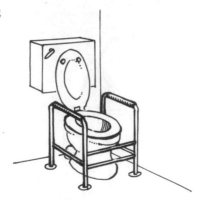

toilet frames

Toilet frames are ready-built floorstanding frames which fit around a lavatory to provide arm supports. The supports should be at elbow height, about 8 inches (200 mm) above the lavatory seat. A toilet frame is useful for someone who can push up from the lavatory seat rather than for those who need to pull themselves up. It is easier to install than a rail, but is more expensive to buy. If you have a walking frame, you could use this instead of a toilet frame.

Some frames incorporate a raised lavatory seat, and some have a spring-operated self-lifting seat designed to help you get up off the lavatory.

Not all frames are adjustable in height. Before getting a frame, it is sensible to work out some of the dimensions required. By measuring the height of the seat and arms of a chair you find convenient, you can gauge the height of arm supports you will need and the height by which the lavatory seat may need raising, if at all. Your local social services department can be asked for advice on a suitable toilet frame and may be able to let you have one.

Some toilet frames screw to the floor and others are freestanding. A screw-down one is safest, especially when a great deal of one-sided pressure will be exerted.

Some frames have extensions to the arm rests: these slope up forward and then level off to give two short rails at a higher level. This eliminates the problem, often found with armchairs, that the arms are the ideal height when starting to rise but are too low to allow the hands to remain in contact with them when the body is more or less upright. It also has the advantage that once you are standing, you can hold the higher rail with one hand while pulling up your clothes with the other hand without having to stoop unsupported.

with a wheelchair

A wheelchair user has special problems in the lavatory. If the two seats are the same height, a direct transfer may be possible. Sometimes a sliding board is needed to bridge the gap or to compensate for differences in seat heights. It is helpful to have a flat surface projecting at the same level on the far side of the lavatory seat to lean the hand on while transferring from wheelchair to lavatory seat. This may also be useful as a place for, for example, lavatory paper.

If there is no room to turn a wheelchair and it has to be driven straight into the lavatory, it may be necessary to stand up and turn round, using appropriate grab rails (or an overhead chain and stirrup) to help, or to transfer forward with both legs to one side so that you can swivel round to face the right way when sitting on the lavatory. It may be necessary to slide forward and sit on the lavatory seat facing the wrong way.

If the doorway is too narrow for the wheelchair, it may be possible to transfer to a narrower commode chair and then wheel this over the lavatory.

There may be other methods to overcome an individual's problems. A therapist from the local authority or from the local hospital should be asked for advice about particular difficulties.

Managing clothes

You may find it easier to manage your clothes standing in front of the lavatory seat with your feet positioned ready for sitting down, firmly holding a hand rail for support. Someone who cannot do this will have to sit on the lavatory, pulling on a side rail with one hand while pushing clothing down off the opposite buttock, and then reversing the process.

A woman may be able to pull up her skirt and underslip, bring them round towards the front and roll and tuck them into her waistband. Trousers or a wrap-over skirt with a back opening are easier to manage. Knickers should not be pulled too far down: they are less likely to fall to the ground if you keep your legs slightly apart. Oldfashioned knickers with elastic at the legs are useful because they can be let down without dropping to the ankles; wide-legged french knickers can just be drawn to one side. A dressing stick helps to push pants or knickers up and down. Cami-knickers which unbutton at the crotch and open-crotch knickers eliminate the need to pull knickers down. Open-crotch pants and tights can eliminate the need to take off further clothing, but good sitting balance is needed while manipulating these. Open-crotch tights need two hands to open accurately. A women in a wheelchair who wears a fully opening wrap-over skirt can undo this and leave it on the chair when she transfers to the lavatory.

A man may find braces useful: these can be looped over his arm to prevent the trousers falling to the floor. Strips of velcro can be attached to the top of underpants and to the inner trouser band so that only one thing has to be pushed down and pulled up. (Spare pieces of velcro should be used to cover the velcro on the pants during laundering.)

Another method of dealing with trousers is to make a back flap opening. Long openings down both side trouser seams combined with a wide elastic waistband to hold the front in position allow a back flap to be raised and lowered. This flap can be pulled up by tapes to each side passed through rings at the waist. With trousers adapted in this way, and wherever there is difficulty, a shirt with a long tail would be better shortened.

It is helpful to have a large well-positioned mirror to check that clothes are in order—for example, that a skirt has been properly untucked.

personal cleansing

Soft lavatory paper requires less effort than the non-absorbent type. Large soft paper handkerchiefs can be even more effective, but should not be used where there is a risk of blocking the drains. Interleaved paper is easier to manage with one hand than a roll.

The lavatory paper holder may need moving to a more convenient position: for example, from the door to a nearby side wall, or on to the wall nearest the good hand of someone who has had a stroke. Paper handkerchiefs can sit on a convenient wall shelf or else be brought into the lavatory in a pocket.

People who cannot reach to clean themselves, may be able to manage by putting a large tissue over a plastic foam washing-up mop or holding it with tongs. (It is easier to use a soft paper handkerchief than lavatory paper.) It may be necessary to practise this technique for some time, before achieving independence.

A horseshoe shaped lavatory seat—that is, one with a front opening—can make cleansing from the front an easier operation. Someone who has difficulty bathing, or is incontinent, may like to have a bidet. Where a washbasin is near the lavatory, it is possible to have a portable bidet, which rests inside the top of the lavatory (after the seat has been raised). It has to be filled with warm water either from a hose or with a jug. After cleansing, the plug is pulled out and the water goes down the lavatory.

It is possible to have a combined lavatory, bidet and warm air drier installed, operated by a foot switch, a hand switch, or by pressing the elbow against a lever switch. This is an expensive piece of equipment but would be useful for someone who has poor balance or limited reach. It is an effective method of cleansing and drying although it may feel somewhat unnerving at first to have a jet of water and then a blast of warm air directed on to you.

Menstruation
A woman whose periods are heavy or painful should seek help from her doctor.

Handling sanitary towels with their accompanying belt and hooks can be a problem for a woman with weak hands or limited reach. Sanitary towels with foam rubber backing or an adhesive strip underneath will cling or stick on to close fitting pants; the tab covering the adhesive area can be peeled off with the finger nail. Towels which tuck into sani-pants are easy to change but leave a relatively small area of pad uncovered and the pants are likely to get soiled.

Incontinence
Many young disabled people who are incontinent as a result of a spinal injury manage this condition so well that it is not apparent. The Spinal Injuries Association book *So you're paralysed* includes a section on coping with incontinence. A great deal can be done, too, to help an older person with this common problem. The Disabled Living Foundation has publications dealing with the problem of incontinence

and suggesting some solutions, and has an incontinence advisor who will help with individual enquiries.

An understanding of the cause of incontinence will help in finding solutions to the problem. Urine may be being passed too soon, before there is time to get to the lavatory. It may happen because walking to the lavatory, managing clothes and sitting down is difficult and takes too long. It may be because the lavatory is a long way away or because the lavatory is cold and therefore a visit is delayed until it is too late. Heating the lavatory and making it easier to use, moving the person's room to one nearer the lavatory or installing a commode, especially for use at night, may help.

As people become older and their muscles less strong, the bladder seems unable to hold the normal amount of urine, and small quantities need to be passed often. This condition is made worse by worrying about not being able to hold out. Making it easier to get to the lavatory helps to reduce this anxiety. Going to the lavatory at regular intervals, even if the need is not felt at that moment, will help to keep the amount in the bladder below danger level. (A kitchen timer could be set as a reminder.)

There is also the involuntary passing of some urine when laughing, coughing, sneezing or stretching, or in some conditions when moving or being moved. For this type of incontinence, a doctor's advice should be sought. Wearing a sanitary towel may solve the immediate problem.

Where there is incontinence at night, having a commode conveniently placed beside the bed may help, if necessary setting an alarm to wake up regularly to use it. Controlling fluid intake by taking most of your fluids during the morning, and drinking nothing during the last hour or two before retiring usually helps. But the doctor must be consulted about this because some people need to take fluids at regular intervals throughout the day.

Faecal incontinence and constipation may be due to medical causes, and a doctor should be consulted. Sometimes, constipation is due to a change in the normal pattern of life. An old lady who goes to live with her children or into a home may no longer have her early morning cup of tea, may get up at a different time or may be unable to get to the lavatory at her usual time because other people need it. Any of these things can upset her pattern of bowel movement, which may be restored if she can re-establish her former routine.

protective pads and pants

There is a variety of devices on the market for dealing with urinary incontinence. It is obviously easier for a man who can wear a urinary bag. Most women prefer to wear some form of absorbent pad, similar to sanitary towels or larger like disposable nappies. Many of these are designed to go with protective pants. Most pads are disposable. It is possible to buy washable pads that can be boiled; they are cheaper and present no problems of disposal. Rolls of cellulose material can be cut up to the size and thickness required by the individual. Cellulose gel pads, which are expensive but highly absorbent, are particularly good for someone with dribbling incontinence. They look like sanitary towels and can be worn with close fitting sanitary pants.

Incontinence pads and pants can be bought from some chemists; they are also available on mail order. They may be supplied free by the local health authority: a health visitor or a home nurse, or a social worker from the social services department, should be asked about this. If the pants offered do not suit you, ask the nurse or the chemist to order something more appropriate for your particular problem.

There are many different designs of protective pants. People vary in what they find most comfortable, most efficient, and easiest to put on and take off. If one design is not satisfactory, try another. Protective pants must always be a good fit, otherwise there is a danger of urine leaking down the leg.

Pants that pull on are suitable for someone who can reach to put them on over the feet. They are also useful for anyone who has difficulty in dressing because there are no special fastenings to do up. Most pull-on pants have pads which are worn inside the pants.

Maxi-plus pants are elasticised with two bands of stronger elastic to hold the plastic-backed pad firmly in place. Kanga pants have an external pouch between the legs into which a pad is inserted. The inner part of the pants is made from material that does not absorb liquid so that urine passes through to the pad. Provided the pads are changed when they are saturated, the wearer stays dry. The pants should be changed and washed daily. They are suitable only for urinary incontinence and are not adequate to wear at night.

Pants with a drop-front panel also enable pads to be changed without lowering the pants themselves. On some people, this panel comes down so low that it may drop down into the lavatory pan.

Open-flat pants are most suitable for someone who cannot walk. Because they open right out, they are easiest to put on to someone who is lying on the bed. They are also good for people who soil themselves badly, because the pants can be taken off without having to let them down over the feet. Some open-flat pants have a drop-front opening which makes them suitable for someone confined to a wheelchair.

Drop-front and open-flat pants fasten with press studs or with velcro or with tape, either down the side or over the abdomen. Openings down the sides may mean doing up press studs against the pelvis which may not be very comfortable for a thin person but are better for a fat person because pressing down studs over a fat stomach is neither easy nor desirable. If it is not possible to put one hand inside the garment to press the stud on, velcro may be better than a press stud fastening.

Some pants are made from plastic material which may crackle and make you feel uncomfortably hot; some are rather bulky under a dress. Pants which are made from a close fitting soft material are probably the most socially acceptable.

clothing

Someone who is incontinent can reduce any problems of clothes washing by wearing clothing divided as far as possible into above and below the hips. This means wearing short upper garments: vests can be shortened to just below waist level, tails can be cut off shirts or sports shirts worn instead. Petticoats and dresses should not be worn because they entail undressing radically if they get soiled. Garments such as nightdresses that have to be pulled off over the head should be avoided if they are likely to get soiled. By keeping lower garments to the minimum, washing will be reduced. Easy-care materials and machine-washable trousers lessen the work. Suspender belts are less likely to get soiled than corsets or roll-ons.

Although wearing separates is better for washing, some women prefer the appearance of a dress. A garment can be made in two halves with the top tucking into the waistband of the skirt.

A nightdress and dressing-gown with open backs make sitting on a commode or lavatory at night much simpler. There should be about eight inches overlap, so that the wearer is properly covered when standing up. A shortie nightdress is also good or a pyjama jacket without the trousers, or a sleeping jacket for a man.

An incontinent man who needs a urinary bag can strap the bag to his leg and have a zip opening on the lower inside of the trouser leg to facilitate emptying the bag.

bed linen
Nylon sheets are useful for someone who is incontinent because they absorb little moisture, so urine can pass through and be absorbed by a pad below without leaving a wet sheet. Nylon sheets are also easy to wash and quick to dry.

Marathon dri-sheets, made from polypropylene knitted fabric, absorb even less moisture. These sheets must lie on an absorbent drawsheet, such as disposable cellulose wadding or an unbleached twill sheet as used in hospitals. Under this should come a polythene sheet to protect the mattress. In some areas, a laundry service is provided for sheets and clothing for the incontinent member of a household. This should be arranged through the home nurse or health visitor or the general practitioner.

An attendance allowance can be claimed if someone needs constant attendance because of incontinence.

disposal of pads
Disposing of incontinence pads and cellulose wadding used on a bed may be a problem. The first thing to do is to contact the department of the council concerned with refuse collection to find out about local arrangements. The majority of local authorities have facilities for collecting incontinence materials, in a few areas more frequently than the normal collection service.

Usually urinary bags must be emptied. This may mean snipping the corner of the plastic sachet to allow the liquid to run out. Pads and wadding must normally be wrapped in layers of newspaper which will absorb the moisture. Some local authorities provide plastic bags.

All local authorities should accept responsibility for dealing with this problem. When a local authority has no special collection service, it should be ask what alternative is recommended.

Some firms which specialise in disposing of soiled sanitary towels from shops and offices, sometimes will collect soiled material for disposal from private houses. This service is fairly expensive.

In country areas, where the local authority may find it quite impossible to help because the people who need the service are too scattered, an incinerator may be the only solution provided it is not a smokeless zone. Incinerators are expensive, and a special type will be required because of the difficulty of burning damp material and polythene.

Bedpans and urinals

Most people know about bedpans, and that there are male urinals or bottles. Some of these are designed to be unspillable. The Reddy-bottle is a disposable urinal made of plastic, which folds and can be carried in a pocket.

There are various designs of female urinals. These save the physical effort of getting on to a lavatory or a commode just to pass water. The Suba-seal, a small, flat urinal with a curved rim that make it non-spill, is small enough to be pushed between the legs without raising the buttocks, and can be used when lying down. The St Peter's Boat has a larger capacity, can be used sitting or half-standing and is particularly useful for a wheelchair user, especially if used in conjunction with a cushion made for wheelchairs (a paraplegic cushion) that has a U-shape cut out of the front for a urinal.

Commodes

Some elderly women use a polythene bucket at night as a substitute for the oldfashioned chamber pot. A bucket has the advantage of being cheap, unobtrusive, and easy to empty. But for someone who is unsteady or who may need to defaecate as well as pass water, a commode should be considered.

You may find it possible to use a commode at the bedside without help whereas getting to the lavatory at night may mean waking up some member of the household. The person who is caring for someone needing help by day will find this less onerous if left undisturbed at night.

Someone who wears calipers or an artificial limb and cannot get to the lavatory without putting on the appliance, may be able to reach a commode. For someone living alone, it may be frightening to leave the bedroom at night to go to the lavatory, or too cold.

Where the commode is in a room that is also used by other people, putting a screen around it ensures some privacy. If someone needs to keep a commode in the living room, it is possible to get commodes that look not unlike chairs and are therefore more unobtrusive and can be chosen to fit in with the furniture.

There are many models of commode on the market: wooden-framed armchair commodes with upholstered seats, basket commode chairs like Lloyd-loom chairs, tubular metal commodes. The wooden-framed and basket commodes are of fixed height (some manufacturers offer their models in different heights) and have fixed arms. Some tubular metal commodes are adjustable in height, with fixed arms or adjustable arms, or no arms. Commodes with no back and two side handles are also sold.

The seat height of most commodes is 18 inches (460 mm)—the height of an average upright chair. Someone who has to get to a commode from a wheelchair needs a commode the same height as the wheelchair, with a detachable arm on one side.

A commode should have a wide base to keep it stable. Unless the legs are farther apart than the arms, the commode may tip.

Commodes do not normally have wheels or castors but it is possible to get a commode with two back castors or wheels so that it can be pushed easily across the room but will not move when in use.

Sanitary chairs are chairs with a lavatory seat which can be either used directly over a lavatory or used with a suitable pan as a commode. They can be propelled by the occupant or pushed by a helper. The chair can be wheeled to the lavatory and, where necessary, moved to the bathroom for cleansing afterwards. At night, the chair may be used as a commode to save going out to the lavatory. If a sanitary chair is to be used as a commode, it must be stabilised before sitting down; if it is not a model with brakes, it should be pushed up against a wall or piece of furniture. The brakes on some chairs are high enough to be easily operated from the chair by hand but others need to be kicked or moved by a stick with a notch at the end, or someone has to bend down to the floor to operate the brakes.

The Easinurse is a specially designed chair seat which has a strategically placed aperture and a bedpan below so that someone can sit comfortably over the bedpan. Some people have difficulty positioning themselves in exactly the right place. There is an Easinurse mattress which is similar.

When a commode is used by the bed, it should be placed on the side of the bed which is most convenient for the user, even if this means moving furniture. If the commode has detachable arms, the arm nearest to the bed can be removed. If the commode is a similar height to the bed, it will be possible to slide on to it. If you do not want the commode right by the bed, put a chair by the bedside so that you can slide from the bed to the chair to the commode.

Commodes can be borrowed from the local authority or area health authority, or hired for a nominal charge from the St John Ambulance Brigade or the Red Cross. Because of limited supplies, there may be a waiting list and there will almost certainly be very little choice. The local authority normally provides a commode only for someone who needs one on a long-term basis. A voluntary organisation should be approached for a short-term or holiday loan. A commode can be hired, from firms in London and in Manchester (no delivery service), or can be bought from large chemists' and surgical appliance shops.

—cleaning

It is important to keep a commode clean. A round steel bowl is probably easier to clean and a bedpan-shaped one the most difficult because the rim which prevents the pan spilling in bed prevents the contents emptying easily into the lavatory. A pan which slides out from the back can be easily removed while someone is still sitting on the commode. If you have to empty your own commode, you may find a small trolley useful for carrying the pan to the bathroom. A length of hose fitted on to the hot tap and reaching to the lavatory helps with washing out.

If it is likely that the commode must be left full for some time before it is emptied, a drop of a neutralising agent, Nilodor, will deal effectively with the smell. If a commode cannot be emptied soon after use, an odourless chemical closet may be preferred.

Chemical closets
In the type of portable lavatory used in aircraft, caravans, long distance coaches and country cottages, chemical is used to deal with the contents which can then be emptied at a convenient time later. With earlier designs, the chemical itself had a smell, but current ones are odourless. Many of these closets have some kind of rather limited flushing system.

There are various shapes and sizes and a fairly wide variation in the price of chemical closets. Large chemists' and camping equipment shops are most likely to stock a selection. The area health authority may supply a chemical closet where there is a need—a social worker or health visitor can be asked about this.

Some closets are small enough to be carried in the boot of a car, others are the height of a normal lavatory. The higher ones are generally more suitable for someone who is disabled, but the manufacturers of most of the smaller ones sell frames which lift the closet up to a convenient height. Most of these frames have arm rests. When choosing a chemical closet, the height of the seat, the accessibility of the flush handle and the position of arm rests should all be considered.

Because a closet can be used many times before emptying, the contents become very heavy. Some models are designed for 60 usages, others for 100 or 120. If emptying the closet is a problem, it may be advisable to choose one with a smaller capacity.

The obvious way to empty a closet is to lift out the storage compartment and empty the contents down the lavatory. But this is not always easy, because the only lavatory in the home may be up a flight of stairs or out of doors. One of the Perdisan closets has an ejection valve and, used with a frame on wheels, can be wheeled out of doors, the ejection valve opened and the processed contents emptied straight into the main drain. (In case your local authority does not allow this use of the drains, you should check with the borough engineer's department before buying this type of closet.) It is possible to use a soakaway. The closet has to be positioned against an outside wall, a hole drilled through the wall for the outlet pipe to a soakaway in the garden. The manufacturers give details of the size of soakaway that is required. This sounds elaborate, but it will eliminate all emptying problems. The closet will still need to be refilled with chemical as required.

One local authority which supplies a large number of chemical closets employs a man whose sole job is to go round regularly emptying them.

Personal care, in the series *Equipment for the disabled,* deals with toilets, incontinence, bathroom layout and fittings, grooming and washing, pressure sore prevention.

You may have slept for many years in the same bedroom and are therefore accustomed to its layout and position, but minor modifications may make it more convenient; in some cases, major changes may be indicated.

The choice of room is important. Another room in the house may be more suitable for you. When it is necessary to get up frequently in the night, a bedroom nearer to the lavatory might be chosen. If you have to spend a lot of time in the bedroom, it should be a room with an interesting outlook and preferably where other members of the household can come regularly without having to make a special trip. One solution is a downstairs bedroom or bedsitting room. This eliminates stair climbing, but only works if there are washing facilities and a lavatory downstairs.

The furniture may need to be rearranged. But if an old person finds it difficult to adjust to changes to a familiar layout, it may be better not to make radical alterations.

For someone who has had a stroke, the bed must be positioned so that it is possible to get in and out from the unaffected side. A bed is much easier to make if both sides are clear of the wall, and good access to the bed makes nursing easier. If one side of the bed must normally be against the wall, good quality castors should make it easy to pull out the bed while it is being made.

If you have to spend a lot of time in bed, it should be placed so that you can look out of the window or into the corridor to see what is going on if you want to. Strategically placed mirrors, like those used on dangerous corners on roads, can give an increased view. It may be useful to have a firm table beside the bed on which to lean when getting up off the bed and heavy items of furniture strategically placed so that you can hold on to them while walking round the room. Big old fashioned wardrobes are usually very stable, whereas a modern lightweight one may tip if used as a steadying post unless it is fixed to the bedroom wall with rawlplugs and screws.

Having a washbasin in the bedroom allows you to take time over washing without keeping other members of the family out of the bathroom. A vanitary unit with a flat surface on both sides of the basin makes it easy to keep washing things, brushes, cosmetics readily positioned and is convenient for someone in a wheelchair. The vanitary unit, or a dressing table, should have a large well-lit mirror, and drawers and shelves to provide storage space with easy access.

light and heat

A bedside light eliminates the risks attendant on getting into or out of bed in the dark. A torpedo switch attached to the bedclothes by a safety pin may be easier than stretching to a light on the bedside table (but it must not be pinned through the flex). Leaving a night light burning helps you to orientate yourself quickly if you have to get up in the night. An additional switch within reach from the bed to control the main light in the room may be an advantage.

A bell by the bed enables another person in the house to be called, if needed. A battery-operated bell, with a suitable length of flex and a switch, can easily be installed.

Someone who feels the cold because of poor circulation, or who takes a long time undressing and dressing, should have good heating in the bedroom. It is useful to be able to switch a heater on and off from bed.

A carpeted floor not only helps to prevent cold feet but is safer, particularly in a bedroom where someone walks without caliper or shoes. There should be no loose rugs, and no polished floor surfaces.

For keeping warm in bed, a hot water bottle is safe enough provided it is not too hot. But someone who has lost sensation in any part of the body should not use a hot water bottle. Some bottles have the cover as part of the bottle, either of pile fabric or ridged rubber. Others should be put into a cover, preferably one covering the whole bottle including the stopper and neck. Filling a hot water bottle may be difficult for someone who is shaky or has the use of only one hand. A hot water bottle holder can be made at home. It should have a hook to take the weight of the bottle, and a bar which compresses the body of the bottle just below the neck to slow down the speed at which water can be poured into the bottle and prevent air bubbles regurgitating. The holder should be screwed to a convenient wall near to where the kettle has been heated, and preferably where the kettle can be tilted on a table top rather than having to be held unsupported. It may be helpful to push something like a skewer through the handle of the stopper to screw it up tightly and to unscrew it.

An electric underblanket can be used for warming the bed but must be turned off before getting in. It is dangerous to have it switched on while you are lying on it. An electric underblanket should never be covered with a rubber sheet because this would make it overheat. Also, it should never be used for drying out a wet bed. An electric over-blanket can be kept on all night at a low heat and would therefore be better for someone who gets cold during the night. A low voltage electric blanket is safer than a normal voltage one. With all electric blankets, the manufacturers' instructions should be carefully followed, and a blanket should be sent back for servicing at least every other summer.

The bed
An oldfashioned frame bed is often more suitable than a modern divan bed. It is usually higher, has a firmer edge, provides better handholds, and can have various attachments, such as a handrail or an overhead chain and stirrup, fitted to it. For someone who has to spend a lot of time in bed, a wide bed provides useful space for a tray or books close to hand.

Modern divan beds are usually between 15 inches (380 mm) and 22 inches (50 mm) in height. A wheelchair user needs a bed 19 inches (480 mm) high, in order to transfer from chair to bed easily. Someone with very stiff hips will need a higher bed. Bedmaking is also easier with a higher bed, and for someone who is bedridden a bed 27 inches (about 690 mm) high makes nursing easier. The best way to decide the optimum height for a bed is by trial. If possible, try getting on and off beds of different heights in the house, or put a second mattress on an existing bed to get an idea of whether it would be easier if it were higher.

It is usually easier to get out of a fairly high bed, one that comes to just below the buttocks: when the legs are swung over the side to touch the floor, you are then already half-standing. Getting into the bed, half-sit on the bed and work the body backwards into the sitting position. Someone who finds it impossible to wriggle on to the bed from the half-sitting position, needs a lower bed.

It is possible to raise the height of most beds. Screw-in legs on a divan bed are normally 5 inches (about 130 mm) high. Some manufacturers provide alternative legs, 8 inches (200 mm) or 10 inches (250 mm) high, to raise the height of the bed (the latter are inclined to make the bed unstable). Three-way or four-way blocks can be bought to put under the legs of the bed. Alternatively, the raise can be made an integral part of the bed by screwing blocks to the bed legs.

Another method of raising the height of the bed is by using an extra mattress. If the mattress is covered in slippery material, a cotton cover should be put over it, to make it stay in place.

If you dress sitting on the bed, you need a bed low enough for your feet to be firmly on the ground, and the thighs supported by the bed during the movements of dressing, so that your body is in a stable position. You may need something firm nearby to pull on to make it easier to get up from a bed of this height.

Various special but very expensive beds are obtainable. Some can be hired. There are hospital type beds, with a wooden headboard, which are a good height for easy nursing yet look similar to a normal bed. There are beds which can be electrically or manually operated to bend at the base of the spine and beneath the knees, putting the occupant into the sitting position. There are beds which tilt upwards until the occupant is in the standing position. There are beds which tilt sideways to change the pressure-bearing areas of the body from one side to the other, and ripple beds and mattresses which also change the pressure areas under the body.

mattresses

The firmer the mattress and the firmer its edge, the easier it is to turn over or be turned in bed. It is also easier to sit down on and get up from a bed that is firm and supporting and does not sag beneath the weight. Someone with stiff or deformed joints may prefer a soft mattress because the body can sink into the mattress and take up the most comfortable position. Most bedding firms make both soft and firm mattresses; some beds with extra support are called orthopaedic beds.

bedclothes

Nylon sheets are too hot and slippery for some people but can be useful for someone who has difficulty in moving in bed and finds the slipperiness of the nylon helpful. If they are fitted ones, the sheets themselves will not slide. Nylon sheets dry quickly after washing. Cotton and terylene sheets, which are also easy to launder but take longer to dry, have a good texture and are cooler than nylon. Flannelette sheets have the advantage of feeling warmer than cotton sheets.

A fitted bottom sheet saves smoothing out and tucking in anew every day. It may be necessary to have help with lifting the corners of the mattress when putting on a fitted sheet. Putting on a clean top sheet is easier if it is unfolded rather than shaken out.

Cellular blankets are both lightweight and warm. They are available in a variety of materials, including cotton. Continental style quilts— bed covers filled with down or terylene—are both warm and light. They have washable covers in a variety of fabrics, eliminating the need for a top sheet. Although these quilts do not tuck in, they stay in place unless you are a very restless sleeper. Flaps can be sewn on to the bottom edge of the quilt cover for tucking in, if necessary. Brushed nylon covers are the most non-slip.

—bed cradles

A bed cradle can be put under the bedclothes to take the weight of the blankets off the feet. To avoid draughts, the bedclothes need to be wide and long enough to go over the cradle and still tuck under the mattress. A bed cradle can be cantilever or hoop design. A cantilever bed cradle allows more freedom of movement because the feet can move sideways. A do-it-yourself cradle can be made with two pieces of plywood fixed together in an L shape.

aids for getting in and out of bed

For someone with particular diffuculty getting in and out of bed, a specially designed hand rail can be fitted to a metal frame bed. This is adjustable in height, and pivots so that it either acts as a short cot rail alongside the bed or swings out at right angles to the bed to act as a grab rail when getting off the bed. The model that slots into position

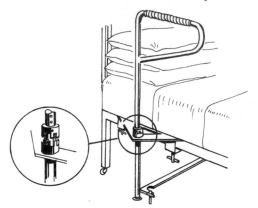

and has to be lifted up and dropped into the next position is more stable than the freely swinging model.

A holder for crutches or a stick beside the bed makes standing up easier and safer when getting out of bed.

A very disabled person may have to be hoisted in and out of bed. The use of a hoist in the bedroom usually entails a rearrangement of the furniture, especially near the bed. There has to be sufficient clearance underneath the bed to take the base of a mobile hoist. If a hoist, particularly a ceiling track hoist, is to be used in both bedroom and bathroom, it may be necessary to reconsider the choice of bedroom: another room nearer the bathroom may be more suitable, ideally with a communicating door.

moving about in bed

Nylon sheets, light bed coverings, an overhead chain and stirrup and an oldfashioned railed bedhead, can all help to make moving about in bed less difficult for a disabled person. Long socks or pyjamas provide a firm grip for lifting paralysed legs. But if moving in bed remains a problem, the physiotherapist at the local hospital or the domiciliary occupational therapist should be asked to help by teaching the best way of moving up in bed, to move to the side, to turn over and to get in and out of bed, and how the person can best help himself. Also, the physiotherapist can be asked to teach someone in the household how to give help with minimal strain to both helper and helped.

—pressure-relieving aids

Pressure sores (or bed sores) occur when external pressure obstructs the blood supply to the part of the body. Spontaneous movement is the natural protective mechanism which ensures that the parts of the body receiving pressure are relieved sufficiently often to allow the blood to circulate in the tissues. People who have lost sensation or who cannot move sufficiently in bed or in a chair are liable to develop pressure sores. The principle of prevention is to change the position of the body as often as a person would normally do it for himself if he could. There are various aids which can assist in this. A ripple mattress helps to relieve local pressures by slightly varying the site of the pressure but does not actually change the position of the body.

Other aids which help to distribute body weight are in the form of pads and cushions. Gel pads are cushions filled with a jelly-like substance, for use in a bed or a chair. Pads filled with polystyrene granules provide another method of preventing localised pressure. Both types of pad are effective only if the person has some degree of mobility in order to initiate movement within the pad.

—sheepskins

Lying on a sheepskin helps to prevent pressure sores. Sheepskins are used fleecy side up. The wool fibres distribute the weight over a larger area and thus reduce the tendency to produce localised pressure points. The deep pile allows air to circulate and helps to keep the skin dry. The ideal sheepskin for this purpose comes from merino sheep which have a dense fleece and soft springy wool. The sheepskin will absorb up to its own weight in water before it begins to feel moist. Synthetic sheepskins, which are cheaper, lose their resilience and also tend to reflect heat back rather than to absorb it. They are easier to launder than a real or medical sheepskin—an advantage for someone who is incontinent. Sheepskins need to be washed frequently; this needs special care.

sitting up in bed

A large pile of pillows resting one on top of the other gives good support, and remains in position better than the more usual way of putting them diagonally. A wedge-shaped foam pillow is available from chemists and shops selling foam rubber. This sits against the headboard behind a pile of pillows, giving plenty of support in the small of the back and at the same time allowing the person in bed to lean comfortably backwards.

Back rests which adjust in a similar way to a deck chair vary in their reliability. Some designs sit firmly in their notches; others are liable to collapse.

It is possible to buy a bed rest which is rather like the back and sides of an armchair. This appears comfortable but in practice is not effective for most people. When sitting in an armchair, the hips are at right angles and the knees are bent. But when sitting up in bed, it is not possible to have the hips comfortably at right angles because the knees

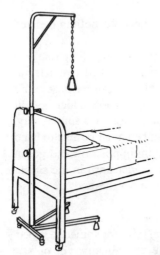

are straight, so the body slides forward away from the back rest, and the arm rests are then no longer in a useful position.

A simple way of preventing a seated person from sliding down the bed is to raise the foot of the bed two or three inches and have a board or a bolster to rest the feet on.

For people who cannot pull themselves up from a lying to a sitting position, there are various ways of helping. A chain of adjustable length with a stirrup handle on the end, sometimes known as a polly perch or monkey chain, can be suspended from a gantry. The gantry should be positioned at the back of the bed because if it is at the side it will be unstable and in the way for getting in and out of bed. Using the stirrup needs sufficient strength in the arms to lift the weight of the body.

There is on the market a spring-loaded pole which jams between floor and ceiling and has a stirrup handle fitted to it. It is easy to install because the spring holds it in position, and it takes up little room. It is quite stable if the handle is pulled in the downward direction but can be dislodged if the handle is pulled sideways, and would therefore not be safe if the person should slip or fall sideways.

Handling the handicapped, published by Woodhead-Faulkner in association with the Chartered Society of Physiotherapy, describes techniques of moving and lifting handicapped people, both in bed and when up.

A rope ladder can be fixed to the end of the bed to pull up on. This can be looped over the end of a bed rail or, on a divan bed, over a metal door handle screwed firmly to the base. A ladder for this purpose could be made with pieces of broom handle or a child's rope ladder bought from a toy shop. A plaited crepe bandage can be used in a similar way. For this method to be effective, the person in bed must be able to bend at the hips, start pulling from the semi-reclining position and go on pulling by climbing hand over hand up the ladder until in the sitting position. Otherwise, one just slides farther down the bed.

bed tables
A cantilever table is probably the most useful table for someone in bed. Unless the ground clearance of the bed is very small, any type of base can be slid under. The table top should overlap the centre of the bed by at least 8 inches (200 mm). This means that for a 3-foot bed (approximately 920 mm), the table should be at least 26 inches long (660 mm). The RICA comparative test report No 11 (May 1972) deals with bed tables.

An alternative to a cantilever table is to have a table wide enough to straddle the bed. An overbed table adjustable in height can be bought, or made by fixing castors on to the legs of a sufficiently wide table.

There are various frames designed for reading and writing in bed, both for those who sit up in bed and for those who must lie flat. Several bed tables, including overhead and overbed tables, are described in *Communication,* in the series *Equipment for the disabled.*

For someone who spends a considerable time in bed, two pockets joined like an outsize oven glove and laid across the bed may prove useful. The centre part should be of non-slip material, such as brushed nylon. The pockets should be made with some fullness to accommodate bulky items, and the openings should be slanted, like a man's trouser pockets, to face towards the person in bed.

Most ablebodied people dress every day without giving a thought to how they do it. But dressing is a process calling for balance, reach, strength, nimbleness of fingers and some stamina. If your disablement makes dressing difficult, there are ways of making it easier. First, avoid clothes that are inherently complicated to put on—for instance, a dress with a zip up the back. Experiment with different ways of putting on clothes and from different positions, if necessary using some form of dressing aid. You may find you have to adapt existing clothes or buy some more suitable ones.

Many disabled people, once they have learnt the correct techniques, becomes very adept at dressing themselves. With practice, what was slow and difficult becomes relatively quick and easy. But if you continue to find dressing a laborious, exhausting and frustrating business, it may be better to be helped with this in order to conserve your limited energy for more important and more interesting activities.

Certain factors increase the difficulties. A cold room makes a slow person even slower. A disabled person who can take only restricted exercise may have put on weight, and tight clothes will then be a problem. Someone who has had a stroke and finds dressing difficult, or who tires easily, should be encouraged to dress before doing anything else. Someone with arthritis may be stiffest and in most pain first thing in the morning, and someone with severe bronchitis may be most breathless then, so may do better by postponing dressing until later in the morning.

Undressing is easier than dressing and, besides being less physically demanding, takes place at a less busy time of the day. If you have difficulty managing clothes, you should start by learning to undress and then progress, if possible, to dressing. Even if you never manage more than undressing, this will relieve a helper of one job and also provide you with a short period of general exercise.

Upper garments are easier to manage than lower garments, because the upper part of the body can be dressed from the sitting position. Outer garments are easier to manage than under garments because they are looser and less close fitting. Therefore, when re-learning how to manage clothes, it is best to start with upper outer garments and eventually progress to lower under garments.

Suitable clothes

The fewer the clothes, the less there will be to struggle into. For instance, a lined skirt eliminates the need for an underslip, and a brushed nylon petticoat the need for a vest. Clothes made from lightweight warm materials are ideal because not too many layers need be worn and they are easy to handle.

If you have poor circulation or need extra warmth because you are slow in moving, you may find thermal underwear helpful. Woollen underwear is still available. String vests are very warm but may be difficult to put on. Button-through vests, with long or short sleeves, are available for both men and women. Ankle length underpants keep you warm. If you dislike old fashioned long underwear, you could consider ski underwear which is both warm and made in cheerful colours, such as scarlet or pale blue. Over woollen underwear, slippery materials or lined garments are easier to put on.

A stretch material for a collar or cuffs can eliminate the need for fastenings. A petticoat or a casual pull-on skirt made of slightly stretchy material will be easier to put on. Stretch materials are less suitable for underclothes and socks because the nature of the material makes the openings small and difficult to locate.

Simple loose-fitting garments with adequate openings and minimum fastenings are best. It is sometimes better for someone who has difficulty dressing to buy clothes one size larger than usual because they may be easier to put on and more comfortable to wear. People who dress themselves usually find front fastenings easiest, especially garments which open right down the front. Someone who has mobile arms but finds fastenings difficult may prefer something with an elasticised or crossover neck. For people who need to be dressed, upper garments and dresses which fasten at the back are easiest for a helper to put on and do up.

—for a wheelchair

For someone in a wheelchair, short upper garments worn with trousers are practical. A jacket that reaches to the seat of the chair but is not long enough to sit on is best. It should be shorter in front, otherwise when buttoned it may ruckle up. Raglan sleeves and plenty of room across the shoulders allow the arms to move freely. Short or threequarter length sleeves avoid soiling cuffs on the wheels.

Trousers cut higher at the back and lower at the front will be more comfortable. They should not be tight in the crotch or at the knees, and the legs should be longer than usual. For a woman in a wheelchair, trousers may be preferable to a skirt because they do not twist as skirts tend to do. Slipper socks are a good idea for anyone in a wheelchair.

Areas of a garment that get rubbed when propelling a wheelchair should be reinforced with pieces of the same material, and two or three extra pieces kept by for replacements.

—with calipers

Leather guards over the joints and buckles of calipers can save wear and tear on clothes. A long zip down the trouser leg seam, opening upwards to above the knee, makes dressing easier with a caliper. The zip usually needs to be in the outer seam so that the caliper straps can be reached. The trousers will last longer if they are lined.

A woman who has to wear a caliper may find that a straight skirt rides up and wears on the metal; full skirts or trousers are better. A long skirt will conceal not only calipers but surgical shoes and a leg deformity, and also helps to hide an inelegant sitting position which cannot be avoided. A wrapover skirt can be made from a length of material with shirring elastic machined into one edge for the waist, and fastened with a trouser clip. A smooth hardwearing lining inside will protect the skirt against friction from the caliper.

fastenings

Difficulties due to an inability to reach a fastening may be overcome by re-positioning the fastening, by moving the garment after it is fastened (for example, doing a skirt up at the front and then swivelling it round to the side) or by using an aid, such as a cuphook on a long stick.

If closing a fastening is a problem, change the fastening. For example, replace small buttons with larger ones, or hooks and eyes with velcro.

Buttons should be as large as possible and the buttonhole big enough to pass the button through without a struggle. Buttons with long shanks and at the front of the garment are easiest to manage. Large hooks and eyes, such as those used on men's trousers, are easier to fasten than small ones; furriers' hooks and eyes are easier still.

Zips with closed ends are easier to manage than the open-ended ones. Where there is likely to be a lot of strain on the end of the zip, it is advisable to fit a longer zip or to put several rows of stitching across the placket and the zip just below the closed end. A fabric tab or keyring attached to the pull of a zip makes grasping easier, and enables it to be closed with a metal hook on the end of a dowel stick.

To close an opening that needs to be pulled tight first, webbing straps can be tightened with special buckles, velcro can be used looped

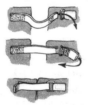

through a metal loop and tightened back on itself, or maternity zips, which allow leeway in tightening, can be used on trousers.

Velcro consists of two nylon strips which, when pressed together, stick tightly rather like a teasel, and are easily peeled apart. It can be used to replace most fastenings. For example, instead of buttons down the front of a dress, the buttonholes can be sewn up, the buttons repositioned on top of the buttonholes, and squares of soft velcro (loop) sewn under the buttons and squares of hard velcro (hook) where

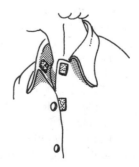

the buttons were. When adapting a man's shirt, it is important to have the hook side underneath because otherwise it may catch on the hairs on his chest. Where velcro is to be used under tension—for example, closing a brassiere or a corset—it has to be threaded through a loop, tightened and then pressed down. A drawback of velcro is that when uncovered it sticks to any material it touches, and picks up fluff.

Velcro is available from haberdashery shops. It comes in a variety of colours, and is sold by the inch. Short lengths spaced out are easier to fasten than long lengths or a continuous strip.

Another useful aid is the Kempner fastener. This is a hook and bar fastener, threaded permanently on tape or webbing. To fasten, the hook is attached loosely to the bar and then tightened by pulling on the tape.

  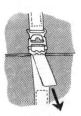

It is loosened by pulling in the opposite direction. Kempner fasteners come in 1-inch and 1½-inch sizes. They are not sold in many shops but can be ordered by post from E Kempner Ltd., 75 Great George Street, Leeds LS1 3BR.

buying clothes

Trying on clothes in a shop can be exhausting and for many disabled people is impossible. Many shops will not send on approval. There are, however, many mail order firms offering a wide range of fashionable clothes on sale or return which can be ordered from a catalogue.

Clothes sense for handicapped adults of all ages, published by the Disabled Living Foundation, gives information on all aspects of clothing and details of many useful items of clothing available on the main retail market. It also contains suggestions for simple adaptations which can be undertaken at home for those who are unable to buy suitable clothes in the shops. There is a clothing advisor at the

Disabled Living Foundation who can be asked about any problems of dressing and suitable clothes.

There is a publication on *Clothing and dressing for adults* in the series *Equipment for the disabled.*

Dressmaking for the disabled, published by the British Association of Occupational Therapists, 20 Rede Place, London W2 4TU, gives information on how to adapt standard patterns to fit particular deformities.

How to adapt existing clothing for the disabled, published by the Disabled Living Foundation, provides sewing notes and detailed instructions for making adaptations.

An illustrated catalogue, *Comfortable clothes—a selection of purpose-designed garments for those with special needs*, available from the Shirley Institute, Didsbury, Manchester M20 8RX (send postage for 113 g), describes garments suitable mainly for the elderly or the incontinent, giving details of the sizes available, prices and suppliers, and includes order forms. It is based on the *Catalogue of garments for the handicapped and disabled* produced by the Shirley Institute and published by the King's Fund Centre, 126 Albert Street, London NW1 7NE.

Dressing

Dressing and undressing are easier if they are planned. Clothes can be laid out ready on the bed. Undressing should be carried out at the same place so that clothes which will be needed the next day can be piled ready as they are taken off.

Some people find that they can manage their underclothes and lower garments more easily lying on the bed. Others prefer to dress sitting on the bed or on a chair and half-stand or lean against something firm when dealing with garments.

There are ways of making dressing easier which avoid external aid. Two garments can be put on together—for example, underpants can be attached to trousers by dabs of velcro round the waist. It is quite easy to unroll or roll up a sleeve by drawing or pushing the arm across the body—a technique regularly used by any housewife who wets her cuffs doing the washing up. The teeth can be used to compensate for a

weak grip or one-handedness—for example, pulling off a close-fitting knitted cuff. (False teeth can be saved direct strain by covering them with the lips first; this is also less likely to tear the clothes.)

For someone with weak arms and shoulders, a dressing stick can be made from a wooden coat hanger by removing the hook and fitting a stationer's rubber thimble at one end of the curved stick so that the clothes cling to it. A notch can be cut at the other end for pushing up shoulder straps, or a cuphook screwed into the end for managing zips.

—overcoats

If putting on an overcoat is difficult because of the weight, the coat can be draped over the front of an upright chair, as if someone who was sitting there had just slipped out of it, with the armholes facing forward. The technique is to lower one arm into its armhole, pull the coat well up over that shoulder and then sit down on the chair while at the same time easing the other arm into its armhole. Someone who has had a stroke should put the weaker arm in first.

A coat made from a lightweight warm fabric, with large armholes, wide sleeves and a slippery lining will be easiest to put on. Large buttons and toggle fastenings are easy to do up.

A loose coat can be got off without using either hand by pushing with the chin, rubbing against a chair back and shaking the shoulders. Sitting on a chair prevents the coat falling to the floor.

—jackets

Someone who has had a stroke will find the easiest way to get into a jacket, or any other front-fastening garment, is to put the paralysed arm into its sleeve first, pull the jacket well up over the affected shoulder and back, so that the other armhole hangs as low as possible and is easily reached by the good arm.

Invisible zip fasteners fitted into the top of the sleeve seam and side seam of a jacket, opening away from the underarm rather like a raglan sleeve, allow plenty of room to insert the arm into the rest of the sleeve. This adaptation is needed only for the second sleeve; the first can be pulled on.

A man who finds a conventional jacket heavy and restricting may prefer to wear a lightweight blazer or a knitted cardigan.

—pullovers and cardigans

A table is useful as an elbow rest for someone with weak arms when putting on a pullover. Someone who has had a stroke should thread the affected arm into its sleeve, pull the garment up on to the shoulder, then put the head through the neck opening and the good arm into its sleeve, and finally pull the garment down back and front.

Pullovers, jumpers and cardigans that are long enough to come below the waist are easier to pull down in position, and are also less likely to ride up—for instance, in a wheelchair—leaving a draughty gap at the waist. A jumper that slips over the head may be easier to manage than one with button-up fastenings.

—shirts and blouses

Instead of having buttons on shirt cuffs, expanding cuff links or two buttons joined together with shirring elastic make it possible to slide the hand through the cuff.

A loop of tape sewn inside the shirt cuff can be looped round the thumb to hold the cuff down when putting on a jacket if the fingers are too weak to grip the cuff. Alternatively, a keyring to which a crocodile clip or a clothes peg is attached by a short piece of string can be hooked over the thumb and the clip or peg temporarily attached to the cuff to hold it in place.

A sleeveless blouse with shoulder seams but no side seams, fastened by two wide tie pieces attached to the back of the waist and brought round to make a bow in front, is easy for a woman with stiff shoulders and elbows to put on.

A generously cut shirt is easier to get into than a tight one, especially when your shoulders are stiff. Some people find it easier to leave a shirt

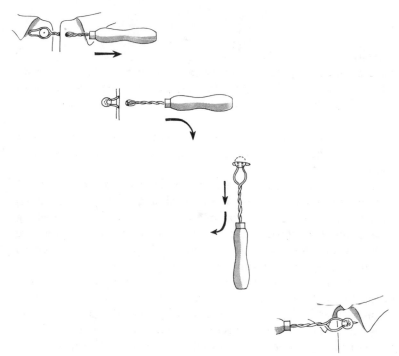

partly buttoned up and to put it on over the head. If it is difficult to do up the top shirt button, a special buttonhook can be bought or made from twisted wire and a wooden tool handle. You have to pull gently on this hook all the time, and swing it round without twisting the handle. If you need to turn the hook a complete circle, a shorter handle will avoid the chin.

—ties

If you cannot manage the complicated hand movements required to tie the knot of a tie, it can be left knotted, loosened to allow it to pass over the head, and then tightened again. Alternatively, a piece of elastic can be substituted for the loop of material at the back of the neck and the tie left knotted. You can buy pre-knotted ties to clip on.

It is possible to knot a tie with one hand provided the narrow end is secured. This can be done by shutting it in a convenient drawer, or by sewing a loop on the end, putting the thumb of the paralysed hand into the loop and using the weight of that arm to hold it.

—trousers

Trousers with a zip fly are usually easier to manage than those with buttons. If the tab is difficult to grasp because of a weak grip, a loop of tape can be fitted through the hole. This can easily be tucked out of sight.

Someone who sits most of the time will find large horizontal or diagonal pockets easiest to get into and least likely to spill their contents.

Elastic braces, either buttoned or clipped on, make it easy to pull trousers up, and also hold them safely while they are fastened. Non-elastic braces are less comfortable and less of an aid to dressing because they cannot be hooked over the shoulders until the trousers are pulled right up. Someone with stiff hips or knees who cannot reach his feet should lower the trousers to the floor by the braces, put the feet into the trouser legs and use the braces to pull the trousers up to within hands' reach. Alternatively, two loops of tape can be sewn inside the waistband just in front of the side seams, and then two sticks with cup hooks attached or two long pieces of tape threaded through the loops can be used to position them in a similar way to the braces method. Or two pairs of household tongs can be used, one gripping each side of the waistband, to pull on trousers.

It is usually better to start putting on trousers from the sitting position and to stand up to pull them to the waist. However, someone who has had a stroke may find it easiest to put on trousers lying on the bed. First bend the affected leg up until the foot is within reach, using the good leg to help if necessary. Place the trousers over the affected foot and straighten the leg inside the trousers. Put the good leg into the trousers and pull them up as far as possible. Lifting the weight off the hips, gradually wriggle the trousers up to the waist. Fasten the fly buttons or zip before sitting up but leave the waist button. It will be easier to put a vest and shirt on when sitting on the side of the bed, so these should be put on after the trousers and the waist done up last of all.

Another method, for someone who has had a stroke, is to sit on a chair and to bring the affected foot nearer the body by lifting the leg and crossing it over the good one. Put the correct trouser leg over the affected foot and pull it up the leg. Place the affected foot on the floor and put the other foot into its trouser leg. Pull the trousers up as far as possible and put the braces over each arm. Stand up and pull the trousers into the correct position. If they are difficult to pull up, lean against the bed, a wall or a solid piece of furniture for extra support.

When fastening a trouser waistband, pull in the stomach to make it easier. It is possible to buy slacks with fully elasticised waistbands and no other fastening.

—*nightwear*

Towelling dressing gowns are available, for both men and women, which open down to the waist in front and from the waist down at the back. This means they must be put on over the head. Anyone spending much time sitting in a dressing gown will find the garment warm because it cannot gape open and expose the knees. The slit at the back allows for fullness over the knees and also helps in the lavatory.

A nightdress which opens all the way down the front is easier for some people to get into. Someone with stiff shoulders or a paralysed arm may find one which opens just to the waist is better. This can be slipped over the head and down to the waist, and then the top part is put on like any other front opening garment.

Pyjama trousers may be easier to manage if elastic is run through the waistband instead of a draw cord. For a man who finds pyjama trousers difficult to manage, a sleeping jacket may be the answer. This is longer than a pyjama jacket and shorter than a nightshirt. Some sleeping jackets are front opening and have a wrapover back slit.

—*skirts and dresses*

A skirt should not be too tight because this would constrict movement as well as making dressing difficult. A long side opening and a slippery lining make it easier to put on either over the head or over the feet. Someone who has to do up a skirt with a zip with one hand can stabilise the bottom of the zip by pressing against a solid piece of furniture. If the opening is made with sufficient overlap, a fastening at the waist only may be sufficient. A wrapover skirt can be placed in position on a chair, so that you can then sit on it and do the skirt up round yourself.

F

A dress is usually simpler to manage than a top and skirt. It is only one garment to put on instead of two, and there are no problems of tucking in at the waist. A button-through dress should be cut with a generous overlap of material at the front, otherwise there will be gaps in the buttons of the skirt when sitting down.

Dresses with a back zip are always difficult. A device that may help, available from most haberdashery shops, is a Zippade, a long cord with a hook to put into the tag of the zip. A sweater dress that has no fastenings may be the easiest for some to manage.

—brassieres

It is easier to hook up a brassiere back to front, then swivel it round and pull the strap up on to the shoulders. Elastic straps make this easier, and for someone with restricted arm movement, a dressing stick will help.

Front fastening brassieres are on sale in many stores, sometimes in the maternity department. Bra-slips are available with front fastenings and also in an elastic step-in style.

Any brassiere can be made to open at the front. The simplest way of doing this is to sew up the back opening and insert hook and eye tape in a new opening at the front. When there is quite a lot of tension on the brassiere, or when it is to be done up with one hand only, Kempner fasteners or looped velcro should be used to secure the bottom edge of the brassiere, and hooks and eyes to close the top of the opening. A piece of elastic across the back shoulder straps of a front-fastening brassiere will help to keep the straps in position.

The clip type of shoulder strap retainer which can be fitted over the front of the straps is easier to reach than the ribbon type attached inside the shoulder seams. Shoulder straps made of elastic or velvet ribbon are less likely to slip off. Elastic loops on a brassiere, buttoning or hooking to a girdle or corset, prevent the bra riding up on someone who uses crutches or who has had a mastectomy.

—knickers and pants

Someone who has difficulty putting on knickers or pants because of not being able to bend down, may find the rubber tip of a dressing stick useful for pushing them down and the end with the hook for pulling them up again. A pick-up stick is another help. Alternatively, some of the methods described for trousers could be tried.

Someone who spends much time sitting, for example in a wheel-chair, needs well-fitting knickers or pants which can absorb perspiration, particularly if there is any tendency to pressure sores. Cotton may then be more suitable than a man-made fibre. Knickers in stretch fabrics are difficult to put on because they cling rather than slide, and the openings are difficult to find.

—corsets

A corset that opens out flat avoids the problem of pulling it up over the legs or down over the head. Also it can be put on while lying on the bed, which makes it easier to do up because the stomach will be flattest in that position. A side opening could be moved nearer to the front, if possible, and made to fasten with either Kempner fasteners or velcro. An elastic loop and button can be added to provide an initial hold before the fasteners are hooked into position. Someone who has had a stroke will need the straps positioned so that she is pulling towards the good hand.

When a corset is fastened by a zip, it may be difficult to put on because it is tight round its lower edge, at the bottom of the zip. There are two solutions: an extra long zip which projects two or three inches below the edge of the corset can be substituted or a second zip can be inserted which opens from the bottom up. Either way, the opening will be made large enough to slip comfortably over the hips. Pulling up the zip can be made easier by putting a hook on a length of elastic or a velcro fastening at the top of the corset, and if necessary halfway up. A loop at the bottom of the zip gives a thumbhold against which to pull the zip.

If a corset is not needed for support, a soft, lightweight elastic roll-on may be manageable. This may be easiest to put on lying on the bed, or can be pulled up to the knees while sitting on a chair and then pulled over the hips. A narrow suspender belt or even a narrow elastic maternity belt may be sufficient. Anyone who lacks sensation should avoid a belt that is tight or constricting. A liberty bodice, although not giving much support, provides some of the warmth of a corset, is much easier for a helper to put on, and supports the stockings.

Back suspenders can usually be moved to the side. This will be important for someone in a wheelchair to avoid discomfort and possible damage to the skin. Suspenders must normally be done up under tension. Detachable suspenders have the advantage that they can be attached to the stockings before putting them on; hooking the suspender on to the corset requires less manipulative skill. Some corsets are supplied with detachable suspenders that slide into a loop of

ribbon. An alternative is to sew a button on to the corset, make a loop buttonhole on the suspender, and button the suspender on to the corset. Another method is to lengthen the elastic and insert a Kempner fastener. The suspender can then be left attached, but can be fastened without tension and tightened afterwards.

—stockings

Putting on stockings and socks is a double problem: holding the top of the stocking or sock open to get the foot in, and then pulling it past the heel and up the leg. A stocking gutter can help.

A stocking gutter is made from a piece of thin plastic sheet curved by soaking in very hot water. The plastic piece should be about 10 inches long by 8 inches wide (250 mm × 200 mm) at the one end, narrowing to 6 inches (150 mm) at the other. The corners are rounded. The ends of a length of tape are attached to the widest corners. Two rounded notches are cut into the sides of the gutter at the wider end.

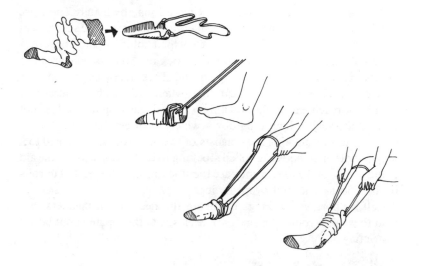

The stocking is pulled over the gutter so that the sole is smoothly over the curved underpart, and the bulk of the stocking gathered into the two notches. The gutter is lowered to the floor by the tape, the toes are inserted into the open end and the gutter is pulled by the tape over the heel and up the leg until within reach. It is then removed and the stocking pulled over the knee by hand. A stocking gutter can be fitted with suspenders for pulling the stockings up the leg (the Red Cross will supply instructions for making one). Someone who has difficulty manipulating suspenders will find a gutter with notches easier to use.

A stocking gutter will slide more easily if some talculm powder is sprinkled on it first. It is important to push the foot well into the stocking before starting to draw the gutter up the leg, otherwise the heel of the stocking will be left under the sole of the foot.

Someone with a very stiff ankle may find it difficult to pull a full-length gutter round the heel. In this case, shorten the gutter to about half its length, rounding off the corners to avoid catching in the stocking. When making or adapting a stocking gutter, it is important to leave no rough edges: use a pair of strong scissors to cut the plastic and smooth the edges with an emery board or sandpaper.

For thick stockings, a rigid stocking aid may be better. These are semi-circular and attached to a long handle. There are three suspenders to attach the stocking to the semi-circle which holds it open. The foot is inserted and pushed straight down the stocking. Some people prefer to attach the suspenders halfway down the stocking, or as far down as they can reach, usually about calf level when sitting. This ensures that the out-of-reach part of the stocking is pulled really tight, but does not leave quite such a long tube down which to insert the foot.

The Roll-on stocking aid consists of two looped rods attached to a long handle. You hook the rolled stocking over the loops, lower the aid to the floor, put the toes in and ease the stocking over the heel. It unrolls off the aid as you pull it up the leg.

Self-supporting stockings eliminate the need for suspenders, but tend to wrinkle round the ankles. The elastic at the top must not be too restricting.

—tights

Someone who can manage tights can do away with the whole problem of belts and suspenders. It may be easiest to put tights on lying on the bed, and is safer for anyone whose balance is unreliable.

Choose non-run mesh tights, of at least 30 denier. Reversible ones without a heel can be put on either way round and the foot need not be put in quite straight.

Someone with stiff hips could try using two stocking aids to pull on tights. A rigid stocking aid would be best with the suspenders attached halfway down the legs. A stocking gutter could be used in the sitting position but the first leg must be stockinged only to the knee, otherwise it will be impossible to get the second leg into the top opening.

—socks

Longer and looser fitting socks are often easier to manage than short stretch socks. Tight stretch socks are unsuitable for someone with poor circulation or deformed feet. Towelling socks are absorbent and easily washed. Tubular socks (without a shaped heel) may be easier to put on if pulling the heel of a sock into position is difficult.

Someone with stiff hips can often manage to put on socks by sitting to one side of a chair and bending that knee as if to kick the backside. This should bring the foot within easy reach. If this still does not enable you quite to reach the foot, you may manage to do so with a rigid stocking aid used upside down—with the semi-circle over the heel rather than the instep.

Another method is to sew two loops of tape inside the front of the welt of the sock about two inches apart: using two sticks with a cuphook at the end, put these into the loops, lower the sock to the ground and then pull it up over the foot. Having the loops in this position helps to open the sock and get it round a stiff heel. For someone who dislikes sewing, two pairs of tongs can be used to grip the welt of socks in a similar way.

Anyone who suffers from giddiness when bending forward with the head low may find it better to put the foot on a small footstool or box when putting on socks or stockings.

—shoes

As with socks, it may be easiest to put on shoes sitting on a bed or chair with the foot up on a footstool to bring it slightly nearer. Someone with stiff hips may manage by bending back the knee.

Shoes can be laced one-handed by tying a knot, lacing from the top downwards, pulling the lace up through the top eye again and tying it in a loop. Elastic shoe laces can be substituted for ordinary laces to turn lace-up shoes into slip-ons, but they do not give as much support. With either method, the tongue of the shoe must be stitched at one side, otherwise it will ruck up as the foot is pushed into the shoe. With No-bows, a plastic device for tying and holding shoe laces, they can also be done up with one hand.

Slip-on shoes, including shoes with elastic side gussets, can be put on by wriggling the foot in, with the help of a long-handled shoe horn. Some shoe horns have a spring between the horn and the handle which makes them more manoeuvrable round the ankle.

Women should wear shoes with a broad enough heel to provide a wide base on the floor. All shoes should be kept in good repair. Worn-down heels can alter the angle of weight-bearing and affect stability. Badly worn soles with holes in them can catch on stones or other protrusions, and trip you up. Shoes with badly worn uppers, and especially felt slippers, not only give no support for the foot, but make walking hazardous because of their tendency to slip off.

Composition soles are both hardwearing and non-slip. This is an advantage for someone in a wheelchair because the feet will not slip off the footplates. But for someone with a shuffling gait or a dragging foot, this can make walking, particularly on carpets, more difficult.

If your feet are inclined to swell, you will be best off with lace-up shoes that have a full-length front opening or sandals that open out completely; the fastenings can be adjusted during the day. People with misshapen feet will find shoes with soft uppers of corduroy, canvas or raffia, which shape themselves round the deformity, more comfortable.

Some people have difficulty in getting shoes to fit because one foot is a different size from the other. Someone with small feet may be able to buy a suitable pair of shoes made up of two shoes of a different size among Clarks odd shoe scheme for children. An alternative is to buy two similar pairs of shoes, one in each size, and get them altered from right to left or vice versa. (The Disabled Living Foundation can be asked for the names of firms who will do this type of alteration.) Although this means getting two pairs of shoes at a time, it allows more choice of style. A voluntary organisation called Sole Mates (29 Hillcrest Road, London E17 4AP; telephone 01-531 3067) has been set up for people needing shoes in pairs of odd sizes.

Surgical shoes are available on the national health service, as well as from private sources, for those who need them. A general practitioner will arrange for an appointment with a hospital consultant to discuss this. Normally, two pairs of shoes are provided, usually with some choice of colour, and should be replaced, on request, as they wear out. Also available on prescription are special lightweight bootees, which are moulded to fit the shape of the individual foot.

More information on shoes is contained in *Footwear for problem feet,* published by the Disabled Living Foundation, and in the Consumer Publication *Care of the feet.*

clothes storage
Someone who dresses and undresses sitting on the bed will need a chair close by to keep clothes on. A slide-out drawer on ball-bearing castors under the bed can be useful for keeping clothes near to hand. Drawers to fit under the bed can be bought with some beds or separately. Alternatively, castors can be fitted under the four corners of a suitably sized box or drawer, and put under the bed.

It is generally easiest to reach drawers that are between knee and shoulder height. Cupboards fitted with shallow drawers of plastic-covered wire, rather like those used in some kitchen units, are good for storing clothes. They are fitted with stops to prevent them pulling right out. The contents of the drawer can be seen through the mesh. Because they are shallow, there is no problem of reaching underneath piles of clothes for the required garment. For someone who has the use of only one hand, or who needs to use one hand for steadying, a central drawer handle is best.

Lowering the rail in a wardrobe or cupboard can sometimes be an advantage. Someone in a wheelchair needs to get close to the rail, and the bottom ledge of a fitted cupboard may have to be removed so that the chair can be driven in as far as possible. Alternatively, a freestanding rail, as in a shop, is useful.

Long-handled coat hangers can be made by screwing a length of wood to the centre of the hanger, rather like a crossbow. The garment is placed on the hanger which is then lifted up by gripping the end of the piece of wood. It needs some strength in the arm to lift.

Bending to pick up shoes may be difficult. A two or three tiered shoe rack helps, or a set of pockets can be hung on the inside of the wardrobe doors to take shoes.

It may help to have a grab handle on the frame of a built-in cupboard to hold on to while retrieving or storing articles of clothing. A clip holder for a stick at the side of cupboards may also be useful.

Laundering

To reduce the amount of laundry work to be done, it may be worth the expense of sending unwieldy items, such as sheets and towels, or articles which require a lot of finishing, such as cotton shirts, to the laundry. Some local authorities provide a laundry service for the incontinent.

Someone from a local voluntary organisation can help by taking washing to the launderette.

washing machines

If buying a washing machine, it is best to choose a machine that can be plumbed into the water supply so that there is no need to attach and detach hoses to taps. All the controls on the machine should be within easy reach and easy to manipulate. An automatic model minimises the handling of wet heavy washing. The advantage of a top-loading machine is that you do not need to stoop to load it. The advantage of a front-loading machine is that loading and unloading can be done while sitting.

Laundry Equipment published by the Disabled Living Foundation gives details of suitable items of equipment that can be chosen.

washing by hand

Washing clothes can be made easier by soaking them in detergent overnight. A nail brush or small scrubbing brush is useful for scrubbing soiled areas such as collars and cuffs. This is easiest done against an oldfashioned ridged washing board, nowadays available in plastic.

Putting a drip dry garment on a hanger is much easier when it is still under water.

Wringing out is difficult for someone with a weak grip or only one useful hand. Wrapping the article round a tap (provided the tap is clean and firmly fixed) and then twisting tightly is effective. Small articles can be rolled in a towel and kneaded to remove some of the water.

drying clothes

Rinsing and wringing is often more of a problem than washing so a spin dryer may be the most useful item of laundry equipment to buy, provided you can manage the various connecting and disconnecting operations involved.

Tumble driers both dry and air the washing, but are expensive. They have filters, which catch the fluff and must be frequently cleaned. These can be inaccessible, hard to remove and difficult to clean. Drying cabinets and heated drying racks cost less to buy than tumble driers. They take longer to dry the clothes and give rise to more condensation, but leave the clothes less creased. Racks take up less space and can be folded away.

A plastic basket on wheels is useful for wheeling the washing out of doors for drying. A clothes line with a simple pulley system can be fixed up to allow loading from one position. As each garment is pegged out, the line is pulled along to leave space for the next.

A rotary clothes line also makes it easy to peg out clothes from one position because it can be moved round while you stay in the same spot. It can be mounted at a suitable height for a wheelchair user.

Pegs can be carried in an apron pocket or a bag hanging round the neck. Someone who finds pegging out difficult should place articles on a clothes line so that half hangs on each side to peg them, even though this way they may take longer to dry.

For someone who has only one useful hand, a clothes line made from twisted elastic cord is helpful: light articles can be hung single-handed by inserting them between the twists. This line has a hook at each end and can be hooked to any convenient fitting points indoors or out.

It is not necessary to dry clothes out of doors. Lines or rods over the bath can be quite adequate.

ironing

It is heat that does the work of ironing, not pressure, so it is not necessary to have a heavy iron or to stand while ironing. Sitting down to iron is much less tiring than standing, although it may take some getting used to. The ironing board must be at the right height for you to sit comfortably with your feet firmly on the ground and slightly apart to allow for a bit of body swing. Many ironing boards are adjustable in height and some are designed for sitting at.

You may find ironing on a well-padded kitchen table more convenient than using a board. Putting up an ironing board and taking it down again can be difficult. An ironing board which folds down from the wall is easy to pull down and fold back after use, but must be carefully positioned on the wall in the first place so that the board is at a comfortable working height for you.

There are many lightweight irons on the market, including some weighing around 2 lb (under 1 kg). Someone with unsteady hands may find a heavier iron better since the weight helps to counteract the shakiness.

The flex is usually attached to an iron to suit a right-handed person. Someone who must iron left-handed should get an iron fitted with a left-handed flex, or one with the cord fitted in the centre of the handle so that it is suitable for either hand. A flex support holder fixed on the edge of the board to keep the flex away from the ironing surface can also make ironing easier.

An iron tidy, which screws to the wall, is useful for putting an iron away immediately after ironing instead of having to leave it to cool. The flex can be wound out of the way round the iron tidy.

Kitchen gadgets and labour-saving devices of good design for the ordinary housewife will also help the disabled housewife.

The Disabled Living Foundation's book *Kitchen sense for disabled people of all ages*, includes kitchen layout and planning, safety, how to overcome difficulties, and advice on diet.

In *Home management,* in the series *Equipment for the disabled,* information is given about a number of aids and adaptations for the kitchen.

Kitchen layout

You cannot make the most of your abilities in a badly designed kitchen. An efficient layout goes a long way towards minimising the difficulties of balancing, moving, lifting and carrying, reaching and stooping, and handling. You should consider the possibility of re-arranging existing units to provide a continuous working surface or building in table tops between units, and of putting up wall shelving which is easier to reach than low cupboards.

The sequence of work surfaces in a kitchen should be uninterrupted. This is particularly important between the sink and the cooker: even a small gap at the side of a cooker can be a hazard, and it is usually much easier to slide hot pans off than to lift them. The continuous work area can be arranged in a straight line, an L or a U, and ideally should comprise work surface, cooker, work surface, sink, work surface.

Someone in a wheelchair needs a circulation space of about five feet in the middle of the kitchen in which to manoeuvre. Others may prefer a compact kitchen where everything is near to hand and the fittings can be used for support and stability.

In an old house where there are steps down to the kitchen or a scullery, it may be practical to build a false floor to give a uniform level.

A door should not open on to someone standing at a cooker or work surface. Sometimes a door can be rehung to open away from the kitchen, or even removed, or a sliding door substituted. Where there are several doors into a kitchen, it may be possible to close one off to reduce the pathways through the kitchen. This has the additional advantage of providing extra wall space for a trolley or shelving.

A window that is not over a working surface is more accessible for opening and shutting. The traditional window over the sink may be brought within reach by fitting a remote control opening device.

working heights
For most people, a convenient working height when standing or sitting is three to four inches below the elbow when bent at right angles. For jobs such as cutting up vegetables and rolling pastry, this puts the forearm in a comfortable working position while keeping the back straight. For stirring and whisking, where the hands are positioned higher above the working surface, a worktop proportionately lower will be easier. A bowl may be better placed in the sink, on a cloth to hold it, when the worktop is too high for mixing comfortably there.

The standard height for kitchen units is 36 inches (the metric standard is 900 mm). Tests on kitchen worktop heights done at the Institute for Consumer Ergonomics at Loughborough University and reported in *Handyman Which?* November 1973, suggested different worktop heights for different jobs and different people.

Where a worktop is only slightly too low, an extra thick board will help when cutting up vegetables or rolling pastry. Keeping the work as near the body as possible minimises the need to bend. A toe recess under a cupboard enables you to stand closer to the work surface and therefore to work with a straighter back.

The work surface beside the cooker should be at the same level as the cooker top to allow a hot pan to be half-lifted, half-slid off the hob quickly when necessary.

It is much less tiring to work on long jobs sitting down. Some working area in the kitchen, preferably between the sink and the cooker, should be left with leg room underneath because it is impossible to sit comfortably at a worktop with built-in cupboards below. Ideally, there should be a working surface at table height or a kitchen table in the room. If this is big enough to serve a meal on, it will save a lot of carrying—and often the kitchen is the warmest place in the house for eating in.

An adjustable height chair with an adequate back rest, castors and a built-in foot rest, is ideal for someone with adequate balance who gets tired standing in the kitchen. A high kitchen stool is an alternative for someone who dislikes the idea of sitting down to work but who can perch on the front of a stool. The stool must have widely splayed legs, which should have rubber on the ends to prevent the stool sliding, and preferably also a back support in the right place to support your back.

—*from a wheelchair*

Someone in a wheelchair will require low working surfaces in the kitchen. If the worktops in the kitchen are too high, extra cushioning on the chair may help someone who does not need much sideways support, provided this does not mean that the handrim on the wheels will be out of reach or the foot plates too low.

Access to a worktop may be easier if the wheelchair has domestic type arm rests on which the padded part stops about 4 inches (100 mm) from the front of the arm rest.

Some cooking preparations, such as cutting up vegetables, can be done on a board or tray fitted on the arm rests.

Kitchen units designed for a wheelchair user need to be low, with space under part of the working surface for a wheelchair, and storage cupboards that can be reached from the wheelchair.

When a kitchen has been adapted for a housewife in a wheelchair, the rest of the family may find the low working surfaces uncomfortable. For many jobs, sitting on a kitchen chair the same height as the wheelchair will be more comfortable for them than standing and bending over a low work surface. Placing a washing-up bowl on the draining board puts it at a more comfortable height than washing up in the low sink.

storage

An elderly person or someone who is disabled may be unable to reach up to high cupboards or to the back of deep shelves. Over-reaching is a major cause of accidents in the home, and reaching down low is not only uncomfortable and inconvenient but may be hazardous because of bringing on dizziness.

Items that are most frequently used should be moved to be within easy reach. Shelves between waist height and eye height are the easiest to reach.

If a shelf is too deep, the back part should be blocked off so that things cannot get pushed out of reach. Storing goods on narrow shelves in single rows means they are accessible, and easily seen. The shelves can be close together because there is no need to leave space to allow articles at the back to be lifted over those in front.

Shelves can be fixed on the inside of cupboard doors. A raised edge or some form of retaining bar will be needed. The door must have strong hinges; even so, put heavy things only at the hinge end of the shelf.

D-handles fitted horizontally at the bottom of wall-hung cupboards makes them easier to open, but if this is not where the door catch is, warping of the door may result. Magnetic catches on cupboards make the door easy to shut but need a little strength to open. Tutch latches need only slight pressure to make the door spring open and a push to shut it.

Some manufacturers make kitchen units with shelves which slide out on runners, and cupboards whose interiors pull out completely like a filing cabinet. Others make cupboards with semi-circular shelves which swing out with the cupboard door.

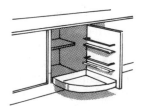

A refrigerator provides readily accessible, compact storage space and enables a variety of foods to be stored for longer, which should reduce the need for frequent shopping expeditions. A summary of the RICA comparative test report on refrigerators (No 1, July 1969) lists points to look out for in a refrigerator for a disabled user.

Kitchen tools such as scissors can be hung on hooks screwed into a wooden batten on the wall. Pegboard with hooks can also be used; it is possible to buy locking hooks which will not lift out of the board. There are magnetic racks for holding knives. Tools and equipment should be adjacent to the work surface where they will be used: for example, food tongs near the cooker.

Polythene or plastic containers with a pouring hole are useful for commodities such as rice, sugar and detergents; the larger containers may be difficult to hold with one hand. The lid should open reasonably easily for refilling. Plastic containers similar to small drawers, which slide in and out on runners screwed to the underside of a shelf, have large handles and are shaped with a lip so that the contents can be poured easily. Small jars and bottles can be stored on a revolving tray so that the desired jar can be brought easily to the front. A vegetable rack on wheels can be stowed under a work surface and brought out when needed.

Plates stacked vertically in a plate rack are easier to handle than if stacked in big piles. A stand can be bought which holds separately four piles of different sized plates in a small space. Cups hung on hooks screwed to the underside of a shelf leave room for other items on the shelf. When breakages are a problem, it is worth considering using plastic cups, saucers, plates and tumblers.

the cooker

With a split level cooker, both the oven and the hob can be positioned at the most convenient height for the individual. The controls can be either below or beside the hob. The centre shelf of the oven should ideally be at the same height as the hob, and there should be a work surface alongside the hob and the oven. Because the oven is at a convenient height, lifting hot dishes out on to an adjacent work surface is less difficult. It is also easier to reach in to clean the oven.

Some people prefer a cooker with a drop-down door because hot dishes from the oven can first be placed on the door. It is easier to lift them up from there than from inside the oven. But it means a longer reach into the oven. Someone whose cooker has a side opening door could use a stool to offload dishes from the oven.

Cooking with gas, there is the hazard of naked flames, and of gas leaking. Modern gas cookers incorporate a safety device which automatically closes the valve when the flame goes out. Nearly all modern gas cookers have grills at a high level, and a grill pan loaded with food may be heavy and awkward to lift there.

With an electric cooker, except when a spiral ring is full on, the only visual indication that the heat is on is the control switch, and the rings remain hot for some time after the power is switched off. The controls on many modern electric cookers are at the back, and stretching across the hob to reach controls can be hazardous. Saucepans used on electric cookers are often heavier and so rather more difficult to lift. However, a heavier pan is more stable and easier to stir in than a lightweight pan—for example, when scrambling eggs—especially with one hand.

Gas showrooms sell special handle adapters to make turning knobs easier. These fit on to various specified cookers but are not interchangeable. There is a leaflet issued by British Gas, illustrating what is available for disabled people. The chief home service advisor of your gas region can be asked to advise.

Some electric cookers, such as the Baby Belling, can be fitted with special knobs which are easy to turn. The Electricity Council has published a pamphlet *Electric aids for disabled people,* available from the local electricity board.

To avoid the possibility of saucepans being pulled off the hob by mistake, a cooker guard can be fitted. Guards are available which are adjustable to most standard cookers and fit like a low fence round the front and sides of the hob. It means you cannot slide pans off the hob—you have to lift them carefully over the guard.

It is unlikely that any cooker, whatever its price, will meet every requirement. Some parts of all cookers are either inaccessible or not safe for a disabled person to try to use. It is worth analysing the cooking methods most often used in order to choose the most suitable cooker. A summary, based on the RICA report on cookers (No 5), of points to look for when a disabled person is choosing a cooker is available from the National Fund for Research into Crippling Diseases.

Which? reported on cookers in September, June and March 1975, and in July 1976, and on split level cookers in August 1974; the report on *Cookers—what to look for* in February 1974 included a section on which control knobs were found easy for disabled users to turn on and off.

When adapting the cooking arrangements for a wheelchair user, it may be possible to have either hotplates or rings fitted as a single row into a worktop of the optimum height. This means the person can reach all the hotplates without having to stretch over. The switches should be on the front edge.

A ceramic hob—a flat glass-ceramic surface with electric elements embedded in it—can be built into a worktop. (The March 1974 *Which?* included a report on ceramic hobs.)

the sink
It is the level of the inside of the sink that is important because that is the working level for your hands. Ideally, the rim of the sink and the adjacent surface should be at about elbow height—higher than other worktops—so that the sink can be at the right height. If the rim of the sink and the draining board are at the same height as the other working surfaces, it may be necessary to have a shallow sink, perhaps 5 inches (125 mm) deep. This is deep enough for washing up and for jobs to do with meal preparation, but not for doing the household washing. Someone with only one useful hand needs to have the draining board on that side.

A shallow sink with no cupboard under it leaves room for a wheelchair, and enables someone to sit on a stool with the legs under the sink. Exposed hot pipes under the sink should be insulated. So should the underneath of the sink bowl itself, particularly for a person who has lost sensation in the legs: a sheet of half-inch polystyrene can be bonded to the base with suitable adhesive.

Lever taps are the easiest to reach, and are easier to turn than a conventional tap. Portable tap turners have a long handle which acts as a lever. A mixer tap with a long swivel spout enables saucepans and kettles to be placed for filling on the adjacent worktop or draining board. A flexible hosepipe which is slid on to the tap can be used for filling buckets and pans.

Washing up

Washing-up machines are labour saving even if there are not more than two people in the family. A front-loading dishwasher is normally easier to use, provided it is mounted at a comfortable height. A dishwasher on the floor may mean too much bending, and one on the working top too much stretching. The best position for most people is similar to that for a refrigerator, with the middle of the cavity of the machine about 40 inches (about 1 metre) above the ground. A wheelchair user may not be able to get close enough to a front-opening machine with its drop-down door. But with a top-loading machine, it may be necessary to remove an upper rack before the lower rack can be loaded, and this may be difficult. The movements for loading and unloading any machine should be tried out by the potential user before it is bought.

Washing up can be made quicker and easier by using non-stick cooking utensils, and also by soaking everything possible, from cake tins and coffee cups to saucepans, immediately after use. A plastic washing-up bowl and a plastic-covered draining rack help to reduce breakages. A piece of plastic foam on the draining board will cushion anything that may fall. Someone who can use only one hand may find it helpful to have a washing-up brush suctioned in place at the side of the sink.

It is safer to do the drying while sitting down, with a drying-up cloth in the lap. Articles rinsed in a second bowl of very hot water will usually not need drying, and can be left in the draining rack until they are next used.

To hold pans and dishes steady to wash them, putting a wet dish cloth underneath may be the answer. An octopus, an oval rubber soap holder with many small suction cups on both sides, may also be useful to hold utensils to the bottom of the sink.

Lifting and carrying

When lifting anything, get as close as possible to it first. It will be easier to control the lifting, and the object will feel lighter, if held close to the body. When lifting something off the ground, either bend the knees or sit down alongside. It may be easier to lift the object halfway on to a chair, and then up. Never lift with the back bent forward and the legs straight. Have the feet slightly apart and one in front of the other to be ready to move forward in the direction of the lift.

A pick-up stick can be used to get lightweight items off high or very low shelves. Cartons, such as those for cereals or detergents, with a hole pierced in them can be lifted up by a cuphook screwed into a piece of dowelling.

It is easier to carry things on a trolley. The trolley should be the right dimensions for the individual user and the kitchen. A trolley can be used to fill a gap in the working surfaces. Most standard trolleys sold in the shops are too low for this purpose but specially designed walking aid trolleys are higher.

An apron with a kangaroo pocket is useful for carrying small articles around the kitchen, and around the house. An apron with a spring clip waistband does away with the need for tying apron strings.

Someone with weak grip who cannot safely hold milk bottles may manage to carry them in a shopping basket.

There is a non-spill tray, taking a cup and saucer, suspended on a handle that requires no exertion to grip. A tray with a non-slip surface and a vertical handle at one end can be carried with one hand and is useful for someone who needs to walk with a stick.

—rubbish disposal

A covered waste bin can be fixed to the inside of a cupboard door. If a strong cord is attached to the hinged lid, passed through a screw eye on the door and fastened to the inside of the cupboard, it pulls up the lid as the cupboard door opens. A waste bin with a swing top is also easy to use. Polythene bags to go inside a bin saves cleaning it out, but may need two good hands to change.

For those who have to take out rubbish for themselves, transporters for most types of bins and even a dustbin trolley are available.

Opening tins

An electrically operated tin opener requires less effort than a manual one and it may be possible to position it so that it can be operated with one hand.

Wall-mounted tin openers are usually easier to operate than hand-held ones because the wall fitting takes part of the strain. The opener should be placed so that the handle can be turned easily and the tin supported. A magnet attached to hold the lid when it is cut off is an advantage. A tin opener with a suction base which anchors to the work surface has the advantage of holding firm without having to be fixed to the wall.

The RICA comparative test report No 9 (July 1971) was on can openers and their use by disabled people.

A special stand to take a wall-mounted tin opener and support the tin so that the opener can be used with only one hand is made by Rentoul Workshops. A clamp can be bought from WAVES (Corscombe, Dorset) which fixes to a working surface to grip the tin while a hand-operated opener is used. There are also tin openers designed for left-handed users.

A sardine tin can be opened with the key supplied even by someone with a poor grip if a kitchen fork or a skewer is put through the head of the key and used as a lever. An ordinary tin opener can also be used.

Opening jars and packets

The Unduit is an opener for screwtop jars or bottles consisting of two metal strips with serrated teeth set at an angle to each other on a metal plate. The screwtop is pressed against these strips and the serrated edges grip firmly while the jar or bottle is turned to unscrew. It should be fixed to the underside of a shelf with the wide angle towards you.

Another device consists of a rubber-covered strip looped into a handle. The strip can be tightened to fit round a jar top: the strip grips the top and the handle acts as a lever to open it. Both hands are needed.

If storage jars have metal screwtop lids, the lids can be screwed or nailed to the underside of a shelf and the jars can then be screwed off their lids with one hand, when needed.

A rubber bottle cap, intended for chemical bottles and available from photographic suppliers, helps to increase grip when undoing a screwtop bottle. It is a hollow cone of ridged rubber which is pressed over the screwtop to give a better gripping surface. Because it is soft, it is easy to put on and off.

Another method, which is very effective but must be done carefully, is to hit the screwtop to make it easier to undo. With a bottle, hold it firmly and bang the edge of the table with the side of the screwtop. With a jar, it may be necessary to bang the edge of the lid in several places, or to turn it upside down and bang the lid flat on the table.

A tall jar or bottle may be held firm for opening by jamming it in a drawer, using the weight of the body against the drawer to hold the jar there, and then unscrewing the lid. Jars may be opened by putting the jar on a piece of foam rubber to hold it, a damp cloth over the lid and pressing down with the palm while turning the lid. Finger grip is not essential provided there is strong downward pressure.

Anyone who has difficulty in unscrewing lids should remind the rest of the household not to screw lids on tightly.

Bag-shaped packets, such as those holding soup or frozen vegetables, can if necessary be weighted down with an unopened tin to hold them steady while cutting open with scissors.

Cardboard boxes of biscuits, cereals and detergents can be opened with scissors or a sharp pointed knife. If necessary, the packet can be held firm in an almost closed drawer.

Heating water and making tea
An electric kettle which switches itself off automatically when boiling
prevents the kitchen getting filled with steam—useful for someone who
moves slowly.

Wall-mounted heaters eliminate the need to lift a kettle full of
boiling water. The heater can be set to boil only a small quantity of
water and this can be fed straight into the teapot or cup. An indicator
light shows it is switched on and a whistle sounds when the water is
boiling.

A teapot is easier to pour if it is placed on something higher than the
cup—say, a flat biscuit tin—and then tilted without lifting. A lightweight metal teapot stand which can be tipped forwards for pouring is
made by Rentoul Workshops (at the Royal Cornwall Hospital, Truro,
Cornwall).

Tea-making machines, usually fitted to alarm clocks and designed
for waking up in the morning, can be used at other times, too. They
save an extra journey to the kitchen after, for example, an afternoon
rest, and also eliminate the need to handle a kettle. An alternative,
which also saves the journey to the kitchen, is to fill a vacuum flask
with boiling water, and use a tea bag.

A milk saver—a glass or metal disc which rattles when the milk
boils and delays its boiling over—put into the saucepan gives both a
warning and time to take the pan off the heat.

Preparing vegetables, cutting bread and carving meat
Preparing vegetables by hand necessitates a sharp knife, which is safer
as well as more effective than a blunt one, and a potato peeler. Left-
handed potato peelers are available. There are various mechanical
devices for scraping potatoes. The ones that work by water pressure
necessitate fitting a hose tightly on to the cold water tap. Potatoes can
be scrubbed and cooked in their skins. They are more easily peeled
after they are cooked: each member of the family can peel his own at
the table, or else eat the skin.

Holding vegetables steady for peeling and cutting is a problem for
someone who can only use one hand, and for someone with weak grip.

A potato peeler and bean slicer attached to a clamp that can be fixed to a table enables a one-handed person to move the vegetable against the blade instead of vice versa.

A board with spikes to hold vegetables firmly can be fixed to the table by a clamp or held with non-slip material, such as foam rubber or a Dycem mat, underneath. A small board with three or four spikes will be suitable for potatoes and other root vegetables, a larger board with more spikes will be needed to hold a cabbage, a loaf of bread or the sunday joint.

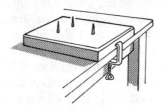

Spiked carving dishes are produced by several firms. Metal ones usually need non-slip material underneath to prevent them sliding on the table.

There are various attachments that can be bought for food mixers for shredding and slicing vegetables. Fitting the attachments and reaching up to feed in vegetables could be difficult, so the movements involved should be tried out before buying an attachment. Storage is an important factor to consider before buying large heavy equipment. If there is no space to keep the equipment out on a working surface, it may be difficult to lift in and out of a cupboard.

An electric carving knife can be a help for cutting bread and slicing cabbage as well as meat. The rechargeable type is the most suitable: it does not have trailing flexes which could be cut by mistake. Using an electrically operated knife is potentially dangerous and must be done very carefully.

A pair of sharp kitchen scissors may be easier to use than a knife for cutting off bacon rind or preparing meat for a stew.

Cooking vegetables

The most difficult part of cooking vegetables is managing a heavy saucepan of water, especially when the water is hot. A saucepan can often be filled from a swivel tap or, if this is not possible, by a hosepipe attached to the tap while it sits on the draining board or work surface between the sink and the cooker. Another method is to put the saucepan on the hob or an adjacent work surface and fill it with water using a lightweight plastic jug or a cup.

A strainer lid with perforations on one side of the lid can be used for draining vegetables in the pan. The strainer lid handle and saucepan handle are gripped together, and the pan can be tilted towards the sink while resting on the draining board, allowing the water to drain through the holes in the lid. The vegetables can be tipped into a colander for a final draining. A better method is to use a chip basket when boiling vegetables in a saucepan so that you can lift them out when they are cooked, leaving the water to cool. It is much safer to slide a pan of cool water back to the sink for emptying later.

Baking

Stirring or whisking in a bowl is easier at a worktop lower than the usual working height because the hands must be some way above the bowl to hold the whisk or spoon. It may be possible to tuck the bowl into the corner of a drawer and hold it in position with a towel. Some form of stabiliser under the bowl will prevent it slipping; a wet dish cloth or tea towel is effective. It may be possible to fit a draw-out flap with holes cut in it to take mixing bowls. This could also be done with a tray fitting across a wheelchair.

Eggs can be broken into a separator which allows the white to run away through a slot to a container below. There are several different one-handed egg beaters with a pressure/release spiral action: as the handle is pressed down, the beater twirls. This requires more pressure but less grip than the usual rotary whisk.

Mixing may be easier with a pastry blender than by hand. A blender has a wooden handle with six wires curved into it in a semicircle with which you blend the mixture. A flour sifter which is operated by squeezing the handle with one hand may be easier to use than a sieve. A rolling pin is effective used with one hand in the middle.

In the RICA report on food mixers (No 12, September 1972), the results are given of tests on hand-held mixers used by disabled people.

Cooking in the oven
Basting a joint of meat can be eliminated by wrapping it in the special clear plastic sheeting or bag which also allows it to brown. This means taking it out of the oven only once; it also saves cleaning the oven.

Oven-to-table ware allows food cooked in the oven to be served direct to the table instead of having to go through the process of dishing up first, and saves on the washing up.

Oven mitts should be specially thick, and long enough to reach beyond the wrist. A disabled or elderly person needs to be able to hold on to a hot dish for longer and to have greater protection against accidental burning.

Putting a baking tray under a cake tin or oven dish makes it easier to pull it out of the oven. Lifting hot and heavy casseroles and roasting tins out of the oven can be avoided altogether by stewing or pot roasting on the hob instead.

Meals

People who are unable to prepare food for themselves, or for whom preparing food is very difficult, because of age or disability, can be supplied with meals-on-wheels by their local authority, often through a voluntary organisation, such as the WRVS. A hot mid-day meal is delivered to the home, for which a small charge is usually made. The number of days a week such meals are supplied varies in different areas and with the needs of the individual. Some get a meal every day, some once a week. The local social services department should be contacted by anyone wishing to receive meals-on-wheels; the general practitioner can be asked to support a request.

Many local authorities, and some voluntary organisations, run lunch clubs where elderly or disabled people can go for lunch. Transport is sometimes provided by local groups. The facilities available vary widely from place to place. The local social services department, a citizens' advice bureau or a council for voluntary service should be able to provide information about lunch clubs and getting transport for going to one. Day centres, too, usually provide lunch and transport.

Shopping for food

Someone to whom a local authority home help comes on one or more days a week can ask for the home help to do shopping or prepare a meal as well as or instead of doing the cleaning.

Members of a local voluntary organisation, such as a youth group or 'good neighbour' scheme, or a church, may be able to help with shopping. The local council for voluntary service or a citizens' advice bureau should know if there are any such organisations in your area.

Some shops accept orders by telephone and a few even deliver the groceries. A strong shelf at a convenient height outside the door makes it easier when taking in the delivered goods. A delivery hatch opening externally for tradesmen's deliveries and internally to the kitchen saves unnecessary carrying. This should have an efficient lock—otherwise burglars, cats or children may make use of it. Some milkmen sell quite a wide range of groceries as well as milk: bread, butter, cheese, biscuits, chickens and even potatoes, can be bought at the door. A plastic-covered wire mesh container for milk bottles, with a carrying handle, is useful. Where bending down is difficult, a wall-hung basket or a shelf should be provided for the milk by the door.

Butchers and fishmongers are usually willing to cut up or fillet meat or fish, especially if they are asked to do this at a time when they are not too busy, or if the customer will call back later.

There is an increasing number of convenient prepared foods on the market—frozen, freeze-dried, boil-in-the-bag. These convenience foods save much of the effort of preparing meals, but are relatively expensive, and some come in packaging that is difficult to open.

When every activity is more of an effort than for the able-bodied or young, energy-giving food is important. Ideally, each day's meal should include a little meat or fish, or an egg, some vegetables, fruit, a bit of cheese, bread and a pint of milk. You should try to have at least 3 pints of fluid a day to enable the kidneys to clear waste products from the system.

Easy cooking for one or two by Louise Davies, published by Penguin Books, is primarily for the over-sixties. It includes recipes for inexpensive meat dishes, and quick and easy dishes. The DLF's book *Kitchen sense* also has recipes with an indication of how easy or difficult each is.

Eating

Although it may not be possible always to plan a menu round easily eaten foods, the bias should be that way. Some ways of preparing food make it easier to manage. For example, shepherd's pie and rice pudding pack well on to a spoon or fork and do not need cutting, mashed potatoes can be host to pieces of bacon; a variety of fillings can be put into a soft bap and eaten with one hand.

It is important to be seated correctly. The most satisfactory eating position is sitting upright in a chair, pushed well up to a table which is at elbow height. This makes it possible to lean over the plate and minimises the distance the food has to be carried to the mouth.

A cantilever table that is adjustable in height can be brought close enough and set at the right height for someone sitting in a chair or in bed to eat comfortably from it. Some armchairs have trays which fit across the front of the arm rests, similar to the tray on a baby's high chair. Other special chairs have a small ledge attached to the outside of one arm rest which can be used for putting down, for example, a cup of tea.

Plastic tablecloths, which are easy to wipe, are available in a variety of colours and designs. Large paper napkins, available in bright colours, are absorbent and can be tucked into the collar. A J-cloth kept discreetly by the table can be used quickly to deal with any accidents which occur without the fuss of having to go to the kitchen to get a cloth. For someone who has great difficulty with feeding, a semi-rigid plastic bib with a turn-up to catch spilt food can be bought in an adult size.

holding implements

Managing eating implements may be difficult and the clumsiness involved may be socially unacceptable, both to the person and to the family. Someone who is anxious about the possibility of spilling food is likely to become tense and consequently more liable to spill.

A common problem is difficulty in holding a knife, fork or spoon. The usual designs are too thin and slippery for any with stiff, weak or unsteady fingers. The most usual solution is to enlarge the diameter of the handle, as for any other small tool.

When an enlarged handle is not sufficient, the spoon or fork could be strapped to the hand. A simple way of doing this is to stitch a pocket to hold the implement on to a band of strong material (for instance, leather or canvas), lined with foam rubber, using velcro for the fastening.

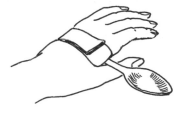

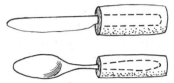

—*enlarging handles*

Sponge rubber tubing, similar to the insulation plumbers put around heating pipes, can be used. It comes in different sizes, with variations in the thickness of the tubing and the size of the hole in the middle. It stretches, and will slide over a handle that is slightly bigger than its hole, especially if it is lubricated with water or talcum powder first. It can be removed for washing the cutlery. This tubing is not sold direct to the public, but it is usually stocked and sold by occupational therapy departments and the Disabled Living Foundation.

Foam rubber, which can be bought in shops, comes in many thicknesses and can be wound round a handle to the required girth, and bound with adhesive tape. Tape with a shiny finish is better than sticking plaster because it gets dirty less easily. The tape should not be wound too tightly because the sponginess of the rubber helps a weak grip.

Bicycle and motor cycle handles could be used. Handles can be bought in a variety of shapes, sizes and finishes; some have finger grips. It may be necessary to cut wedges from a cork and force them into the gap round the shaft of the fork or other tool so that the cycle handle holds it firmly in place.

Balsa wood can be used to make lightweight enlarged handles: two pieces of balsa wood can be clamped together (or held together with elastic bands) with the tool between, and glued. Flat-handled tools such as forks, spoons and nail files will make their own indentation in the wood, larger tools such as knives may need a groove cut first. Balsa is easy to shape to a final rounded handle and should be given a protective coat of balsa paint. The handle should not be allowed to get too wet.

Plastic handles for chisels are available in various sizes, and a home handyman should be able to fix one of these on to a cut-off knife, fork or spoon.

Several firms supply knives, forks and spoons with enlarged handles, or will fit soft padded handles on to forks and spoons sent to them.

—special cutlery

Cutting up food normally entails holding it firmly with a fork and using a sawing action with the knife. This may be difficult for someone with weak grip in either hand, and will be impossible for someone who has the use of only one hand after a stroke. A knife with a sharp curved cutting edge will cut food with firm downward pressure followed by a rocking movement to lengthen the cut. The cutting edge should be kept very sharp; trying to cut with a knife requires much more effort and may not work. There is the Manoy knife with a short curved blade, and the Nelson knife which has a longer curved blade and prongs at the

end, similar to a cheese knife, so that it can be used as a fork, too. But a sharp edge near the prongs could easily cut the mouth so it is safer to cut off a piece of food, put down the knife and eat with an ordinary fork, american fashion.

The Manoy spoon has been designed primarily for people with arthritis: the bowl of the spoon is angled so that it can be used by someone with a stiff hand and limited wrist movement. The handle is thicker than average. Right and left handed spoons are made.

Someone who has a severe tremor may find a weighted cuff like a sandbag bracelet reduces the effect of this tremor. Someone who has two stiff elbows but reasonably agile hands may manage with light-weight long-handled cutlery.

Some occupational therapy departments have facilities for making implements to suit an individual's requirements, and to try them out.

stabilising plates and other equipment

Someone who has difficulty cutting up food may exert so much force that the plate gets pushed along the table. A non-slip mat under a plate will prevent this. Such mats can be used in many other situations: for example, stabilising a mixing bowl or the telephone. They are especially needed by someone who is effectively one-handed after a stroke.

Mats can be made from Dycem, a gelatinous substance which is non-slip on both sides. Dycem can be bought in lengths or as mats either $8\frac{1}{2}$ inches (210 mm) or 10 inches (250 mm) in diameter. To work effectively, Dycem must be clean, dust-free and dry.

Pimple rubber, as used on table tennis bats, is suitable to stick or sew to any surface that would otherwise be slippery. Two circles cut out and stuck back to back will make a table mat which prevents both the plate and the mat slipping. (Pimple rubber can also be glued round surfaces such as a slippery handrail to give a better grip.)

Latex mesh carpet underlay can be made into non slip mats. A small square could be folded up and carried in a pocket or handbag to use, for example, under a plate in a restaurant.

To make the whole surface of a table or desk non-slip, limpet cloth, a cotton-backed cloth with a non-slip surface, can be cut to size and stuck on. This only works if it is dry and free of dust.

keeping food on the plate

The Manoy plate is shaped so that food can be pushed against the inside edge and scooped up easily on the spoon or fork. The edge acts as a built-in buffer. It is made from lightweight melamine and comes in various sizes.

A dish with a rim is better than a flat plate. Plate surrounds, plate guards and clip-on plate clamps can be fitted on to an ordinary plate to prevent food being pushed off the plate.

G

Deep soup bowls with almost vertical sides are easier to use than the traditional flat soup plate. Soup is easiest drunk from a beaker.

A plastic egg cup is obtainable which has a suction base to grip the plate. Or an egg cup with an attached plate base could be used.

Someone who has the use of only one hand can spread butter on a slice of bread by using a short knife grasped in the fingers while the bread is held down by the thumb. The action is rather similar to that of using a potato peeler. Alternatively, bread can be buttered while pushing the slice into the corner of a tray. It may be easier to butter the bread while the loaf is held on a spiked board for slicing or with a slice of bread held on the shorter spikes of a spiked carving dish.

keeping food warm
Eating may be such a slow process that food gets unappetisingly cold. A fireproof plate which can be heated up in the oven before the meal or a plate with a hot water compartment underneath will keep food warm longer. The latter are mostly produced for children but not all are decorated with flopsy bunnies.

The Bambinette is a dish with an electrically heated base, thermostatically controlled. Or a small electrically heated tray, designed to keep a vegetable dish warm for second helpings, could be put under a plate. It should have thermostatic control and be set to a low heat, otherwise the food would remain too hot to eat. Or a hot plate warmed by a nightlight could be used. An insulated beaker or mug can be bought for keeping drinks hot.

Drinking
Drinking without help is often possible when eating is not. This should be turned to advantage: soups, stews and suitable puddings can be taken from a beaker even if they do need chewing. It may be preferable to drink a liquidised meal rather than having to be fed with it in its normal state.

Cups with handles are easier to hold. Many soup cups are made with two handles, and a few tea services have two-handled cups. Two-handled plastic mugs can also be bought.

The Manoy beaker, made of lightweight melamine, has a cutaway stem so that it can be lifted with the palm as well as gripped with the fingers of both hands. It can also be gripped between the thumb and first finger.

A swivelling cup on an adjustable stand which can be tipped forward for drinking and returns to the upright position when released by the lips enables someone to drink without using the hands.

Someone who is unable to handle a beaker may be able to drink through a straw or a plastic tube. Bendable straws are useful. The longer the drinking tube, the harder the work to suck the liquid up. So if you cannot bend to get down to the beaker, put the beaker on something higher rather than having a long drinking tube. A drinking tube can be attached to the side of a beaker by one of those metal clips designed to clip a pen into a jacket pocket. A heavy squat beaker should be used so that it is not easily overturned.

Someone who is liable to knock over even the sturdiest glass may find a cyclist's drinking bottle is safer. This has a lid and therefore the liquid cannot be spilt but the base is rounded so the bottle may need to be held securely in a stable container.

Feeding cups with spouts are available in various designs for those who are unable to drink without help or who have to drink lying down. One type has two side handles, another is made with a narrow spout for liquids and a wider spout for purées.

There are many national and local clubs and groups for specific activities which anyone can join. It is worthwhile forging links with any local organisation that meets regularly, such as the Women's Insitute or Townswomen's Guild, a chess club, a bridge club, an art club. Most adult education colleges make special provision for disabled people to attend classes.

There are also specialist groups for activities for disabled people both in and out of the home. Many of these have been started by disabled people who were enthusiastic enough to follow up their own interests and abilities.

Correspondence and companionship clubs

There are a number of small organisations which aim to alleviate the isolation of disabled people and those who look after a disabled or elderly person. Some keep in touch with their members by circulating taped material on cassettes.

Wider Horizons, an organisation which links its members through a magazine, *W.H.*, aims to promote wider interests among disabled and housebound people and tells them of new organisations and developments. Contact Miss V Dench, 12 Birchwood Road, London SW17 9BQ for information. The Joint Involvement Mutual Society (J.I.M.S.) produces a newsletter and a magazine and provides telephone and correspondence contacts. The chairman is Mrs J M Butchard, White Rails, 86 Turnpike Road, Aughton, Lancashire.

Stamp collecting and puzzles

Collecting stamps can be a satisfying hobby for a housebound person, and contacts can be made with stamp collectors elsewhere. A pamphlet *Let's collect stamps* is sold by The Stamp Collecting Promotion Council, 47 Southampton Way, London SE5 7SW. Competitions and crosswords can be enjoyed by some disabled people—to the point of mania. Free-entry prize crosswords are published in many daily and sunday newspapers and magazines. The weekly *Competitors Journal* includes news and results of competitions and its own contests. There are also monthly magazines of quizzes, puzzles and competitions.

Some people find doing jigsaw puzzles a relaxation and an interesting way of passing the time. It is possible to borrow jigsaw puzzles from the British Jigsaw Puzzle Library (Mrs B Beves, Old Homend, Stretton Grandison, Ledbury, Herefordshire HR8 2TW); there is an annual subscription.

Printing
A number of housebound disabled people have bought small printing presses which enable them to produce printed letterheads, invitation cards, trade cards, and similar work. The British Printing Society, established for amateur printers, produces a monthly magazine, and has an advisory bureau and a postal library service for members. There is an assistant secretary for disabled printers: Mr A F Turner, 38 North Drive, Orpington, Kent BR6 9PQ.

Photography
Some local associations for the disabled run photographic competitions, and local photographic societies may also welcome and help disabled members.

The secretary of a charity called 'Photography for the Disabled' (190 Secrett House, Ham Close, Ham, Richmond, Surrey TW10 7PE), will advise on photographic equipment suitable for disabled people; for example, an adapted camera has been devised to fit on to a wheelchair.

Amateur radio
A number of disabled people confined to their homes have become enthusiastic about radio—either listening to broadcasting and amateur stations all over the world or widening their interest by qualifying for an amateur transmitting licence.

A leaflet, *How to become a radio amateur*, is available from the Home Office, Radio Regulatory Division, Licensing Branch (Amateur), Waterloo Bridge House, Waterloo Road, London SE1 8UA. The annual licence fee for a radio transmitter is £4·80.

Equipment need not be expensive and the Radio Amateur Invalid and Bedfast Club (57 Pantain Road, Loughborough, Leicestershire) will advise and assist disabled people. The Radio Society of Great Britain (35 Doughty Street, London WC 1N 2AE) also helps either directly or through its members. Publications are available to explain the techniques of listening and transmitting.

Music

Music can become a source of enjoyment even to someone who has not formerly shown much interest. For listening at home, a radio set is in some circumstances provided by the local social services department. Records are loaned by many public libraries in the same way as books. A lot of music nowadays is recorded on tape and can be bought in the form of a cassette or cartridge and played back on a machine which may be easier to manipulate than a record player.

Some concert halls make it easy for disabled people to go to concerts by having easy access from cars, nearby parking facilities, good lifts and a special area in the hall for wheelchairs. Under the Chronically Sick and Disabled Persons Act 1970, all new buildings to be used by the public, which includes concert halls, must be built so that disabled people can get into them, and also can use their lavatory and parking facilities. (But a disabled person may find that even if the lavatories are accessible, there is not sufficient time to use them during the interval, because of being slower getting to and fro, and so many other people wanting to use the lavatory.)

Someone who plays, or wants to play, a musical instrument may have to have this adapted so that he can play it despite his handicap. REMAP, an organisation with panels of engineers throughout the country, can be asked to make special adaptations to musical instruments for individual needs. The address is Rehabilitation Engineering Movement Advisory Panels, Thames House North, Millbank, London SW 1P 4QG.

A book for teachers of music to handicapped children, *They can make music* by Philip Bailey (Oxford University Press), includes sections on gadgets and adaptations, and could also be suitable for adults. A report on a study conference held in 1970 on music and the physically handicapped, published by the Disabled Living Foundation, gives further information on this subject.

Pets

Someone who has never kept a pet may not realise that the affection shown by a small dog or cat can go a long way towards compensating for lack of human companionship. Even a small dog needs some exercising; taking a dog out for a daily short walk encourages a disabled or elderly person to take exercise, too, and to talk to other dog owners.

A budgerigar or even a goldfish would be another possible pet. Birds and cages for someone disabled or an elderly person living alone can be obtained through the Companionship Trust (secretary: J Kuttner, 58 Broadwalk, London E18).

Bird watching

People who are confined to the house for much of the time can get a great deal of pleasure out of watching birds, even in a town. A net bag of nuts hung outside the window, a feeding trough on a spike stuck in the lawn or on a hook outside the window frame or a feeding dish held to the window pane by a suction cup, will encourage birds to come.

Books and leaflets about birds, their study and conservation, are available from the Royal Society for the Protection of Birds, The Lodge, Sandy, Bedfordshire SG19 2DL. At some of the RSPB bird reserves there are facilities for disabled visitors.

Gardening

A garden can be adapted to make it easier for a disabled or elderly person to manage, perhaps by changing the layout or building raised flower beds. There are tools that reduce the amount of stooping, reaching and bending, and special lightweight tools. Ways of making the work easier are sitting down to some jobs that are usually done standing, changing jobs frequently so that it is not necessary to stay in one position for a long time, not doing too much and stopping before getting tired. Someone who has not got a garden can still be a gardener with window boxes and house plants.

The easy path to gardening, published by the Reader's Digest Association in conjunction with the Disabled Living Foundation, is a book intended for people who because of disability or age can no

longer garden in the way they used to. For instance, it gives advice on
suitable tools and on mowing a lawn from a wheelchair. It is also for
people who have had little previous experience of gardening, and gives
advice to people who are approaching old age or have a progressive
condition and want to prepare an easily managed garden for the time
when they become less fit.

At the Gardening Centre, Syon Park, Brentford, Middlesex, there is
a demonstration garden for the disabled and elderly. This includes
raised beds and other suggested ways of planting, a greenhouse which
allows entry for a wheelchair and has propagating shelves within easy
reach, and a selection of suitable garden tools. Demonstrations can be
arranged on wednesdays and fridays, preferably by appointment.
There is also a garden designed for the disabled at Battersea Park in
London, and one is being created at the RHS gardens at Wisley.

The Garden Club (affiliated to the Gardens for the Disabled Trust)
has been formed to enable disabled gardeners to share their interest.
The national secretary is Mrs H D Challen, Lilac House, Biddenden,
Kent.

Leisure and gardening is a publication in the series *Equipment for
the disabled.*

Sports and physical recreation

Disabled people are able to take part in a wide range of sporting activities.

There are many national organisations concerned with sport for the disabled: for instance, a Scottish and a Welsh Sports Association for the Disabled, an English Paraplegic Sports Association and similar organisations in Northern Ireland, Scotland and Wales. There is a National Association of Swimming Clubs for the Handicapped, a National Wheelchair Basket Ball League, a Riding for the Disabled Association, a Society of One-Armed Golfers.

Holidays with sailing facilities for handicapped people are provided at the Christian Sailing Centre, Newport, Isle of Wight. 'Sparkle' is a catamaran, designed to take people in wheelchairs, built and maintained by Sparks ('Sportsmen pledged to aid research into crippling', 27 Oxford Street, London W 1) who take disabled people for trips on her.

Some national associations for disabled people include physical recreation in their programmes, such as the British Limbless Ex-Service Men's Association, and PHAB (physically handicapped and abled bodied) clubs and residential courses.

At Stoke Mandeville in Buckinghamshire there is a specially equipped sports stadium and the national Stoke Mandeville Games for the Paralysed are held there every year (so are the international Games in non-Olympics years), and also the British Sports Association for the Disabled's annual multi-disabled games. The British Commonwealth Paraplegic Games are staged every two years in different countries.

There are many local sports clubs for the disabled throughout the country, and local authorities in some areas provide good facilities, particularly for swimming. Any disabled person wanting to know about clubs and facilities in the area in which he lives should write to the British Sports Association for the Disabled, Harvey Road, Aylesbury, Buckinghamshire, or to the Disabled Living Foundation. *Outdoor pursuits for disabled people,* published by the DLF, includes addresses of organisations, clubs and authorities able to give advice and information.

A substantial proportion of people with all kinds of physical disabilities have significant sexual problems. Sometimes these are connected directly with the disorder of the sexual system; but difficulty may stem from other causes—for example, arthritis may make the movements of sexual intercourse difficult or impossible. The problems tend to increase with the severity of the disability. There is no need to feel that you are in any way odd because you have sexual problems—many people who are not disabled at all have problems with their sex life.

Many sexual difficulties can be solved or ameliorated by factual information or advice. When problems are mainly mechanical or concerned with comfort or safety, these may be solved by advice on alternative techniques and positions for intercourse. Aids to help with sexual activity and intercourse include pads, cushions, and coverings for external stoma. There are also prostheses ranging from minor fittings or attachments to help achieve an erection or penetration to a substitute or artificial penis and vibrators. The Disabled Living Foundation plans to have a section concerned with sexual aids and problems of the disabled in its display centre in London. Where sexual intercourse is impossible, advice can be sought on non-coital sex.

Emotional problems arising from or causing sexual difficulty are sometimes serious and complicated. Personal counselling, perhaps over a long period, may be needed.

Sex education for young handicapped people, particularly those in residential homes and schools, should provide not only the type of information that is appropriate to all adolescents but additional advice relevant to the individual's disability.

There has been a common misapprehension that disabled people should not expect to have a sex life. On the contrary: someone who is deprived in other areas of living may have a greater need for the emotional and physical satisfaction of sexual contact. Many disabled people lead satisfying and exciting sex lives and bring up babies very successfully. Even in long-stay sheltered accommodation, where one of the problems is lack of privacy, the attitudes of the staff can help to overcome problems.

Although the sexual urge may decrease with age, sex can be not only possible but enjoyable for elderly people, and an older disabled person should not hesitate to ask for advice.

The Committee on Sexual Problems of the Disabled (SPOD) commissioned RICA to do research into this subject. (Their report *Sex and the Physically Handicapped* has been published by the National Fund for Research into Crippling Diseases.) SPOD gives factual help and information, and refers people for further advice or counselling if possible in the area where they live. Enquiries should be made in writing to SPOD at 183 Queensway, London W2 5HL, giving as full details of the specific problem as possible. SPOD is producing pamphlets, in cooperation with the relevant organisations, to help specific disability groups: spastics, those with spina bifida, those with multiple sclerosis. Also, a series of SPOD advisory leaflets is available, dealing with particular problems and solutions.

Entitled to love is a book on the sexual and emotional needs of the handicapped by Dr Wendy Greengross, published by Malaby Press in association with the National Fund for Research into Crippling Diseases. *Sexual options for paraplegics and quadriplegics,* published by Little, Brown (available from Quest Publishing Agency, Beckenham, Kent) explains some of the possibilities and methods, giving explicit directions with close-up photographs. *So you're paralysed,* published by the Spinal Injuries Association, a booklet dealing with the problems of the paraplegic person, has a section on sex for both men and women, and on pregnancy and birth control.

—genetic counselling
Disabled people who are worried about whether there is a danger that their children may inherit a similar disability should seek genetic counselling. Where there is a possible risk, the general practitioner can refer the couple to one of the genetic counselling centres which exist in some of the larger cities throughout the country. At such a centre, the likely risk of a child being handicapped can be assessed and explained.

Since the Chronically Sick and Disabled Persons Act 1970, where practicable all new buildings to be used by the general public must be built so that disabled people can get into them and so that they can use their car parking and lavatory facilities; public lavatory facilities must be accessible to disabled people; premises such as hotels, restaurants and theatres must have specially signposted lavatory facilities for the disabled. In theory, this is excellent, in practice, it will take both time and money and some authorities are prepared to spend money in this way and others are not. In some places where access is provided, it means going through a back door or up a service lift.

There is a need for planning authorities to think in terms of the total environment rather than isolated areas in regard to the handicapped. So often a considerable amount of work has been done in individual buildings but the environmental planners have still left considerable barriers to, for instance, wheelchair users. New towns could take the opportunity to plan in a global manner—after all, what is good for the wheelchair user is good for the mother with a pram. There should also be provision for the disabled person not in a wheelchair who can walk only short distances and cannot walk up a ramp.

Guides to access
Guide books have been produced, in conjunction with the Central Council for the Disabled (and available from the CCD), for over 70 towns and cities throughout the country, giving information about access to local shops, lavatories, restaurants, cinemas, hotels and public buildings. These books are designed to help both people living there and visitors. A few guides cover a wider area than just a town— such as the one on Gloucestershire and those on easy access sightseeing in Dorset and Sussex.

There are also more specialist guide books published by the CCD: *Access to theatres and cinemas in central London for people in wheelchairs,* for example, and *Access to public conveniences—a handbook for the disabled person* covering London and the rest of the country. *A guide to London's underground stations—a handbook for the disabled person* is particularly useful for those who find stair climbing a problem. Freda Bruce Lockhart's *London for the Disabled,* published by Ward Lock, is another useful book.

Anyone who would like to start compiling a guide to access in their locality can get instructions for doing this from the Central Council for the Disabled, 34 Eccleston Square, London SW1V 1PE.

The National Trust's annual information booklet for visitors to Trust properties indicates those accessible to wheelchairs and those providing wheelchairs. Some art galleries and museums loan wheelchairs to go round in to look at the exhibits. The *Good Food Guide,* published by the Consumers' Association, indicates which restaurants are accessible to wheelchair users. The Automobile Association's *Guide for the disabled* indicates hotels with suitable accessibility in the United Kingdom and Eire, together with facilities in motorway service areas. The Royal Automobile Club's guide and handbook indicates ground floor bedrooms and facilities in hotels, and if there are steps to negotiate. The Wales Tourist Board has a free guide for disabled visitors to Wales.

Holidays

A holiday for an elderly person or someone who is disabled may be provided by or subsidised by the local authority. It is not always possible for everyone who wants to go on holiday to be fitted in every year so anyone wanting a holiday should contact the local social services department well in advance. Help is also available for getting to the holiday; local authorities either hire coaches or conduct parties by rail. Voluntary bodies, such as the WRVS, and also sometimes the hospital car service, may be brought in to help. In many cases, voluntary associations, acting as agents for the local authority, take over responsibility for organising and running holidays for disabled or elderly people, including holidays abroad. *Holiday Which?* February 1976 included a report on holiday information for the disabled.

A few local authorities subsidise the holiday of someone who is escorting and looking after the disabled or elderly person. One or two local authorities provide or subsidise a holiday for someone who spends the rest of the year tied to the house looking after a disabled or elderly person, and may make arrangements for that person to go into a residential home, or to hospital, for the week or two.

For those who want to make their own arrangements, *Holidays for the physically handicapped,* published by the Central Council for the Disabled, is a guide to holiday homes, camps, guesthouses, hotels and private addresses which provide accommodation for the disabled. The types of accommodation and those for whom it caters are listed, and so are voluntary organisations, including those concerned with specific disabilities, which are able to give practical help. The holiday organiser at the Spastics Society will help with holidays for people with cerebral palsy. The British Rheumatism and Arthritis Association runs four seaside hotels which have been specially adapted. The Disabled Drivers' Association has a holiday centre at Ashwellthorpe Hall, Norfolk.

For someone who wants to holiday abroad, the Automobile Association's *Guide* lists organisations in 16 continental countries who give travel advice to handicapped visitors. *Access in Paris,* a tourist guide for the disabled, is available from the Central Council for the Disabled.

Members of the Disabled Drivers' Association and of the Disabled Drivers' Motor Club may be eligible for concessions for their vehicles on some sea ferries; details of these arrangements and information about suitable places for holidays can be obtained from the office manager of the DDA and the secretary of the DDMC.

A disabled person may have difficulty in getting holiday insurance at normal rates; the Central Council for the Disabled has an arrangement for a special master policy.

Air travel

Someone who has difficulty in walking or relies on the use of a wheelchair, or who is disabled in some other way, should find out before making a booking what assistance the airlines on that route offer for a handicapped passenger, such as an ambulance or wheelchair at the airport, and whether any charge will be made for these special arrangements. Remember to check what provision will be made at airports en route and at your destination as well as at the airport of departure. At some airports, corridors project from the airport building right into the aircraft itself; others have escalators or moving pavements. But in some, passengers have to climb up a lot of steps— this can tax even the ablebodied.

At most airports, it is possible to borrow a wheelchair. A request should be made through the airline when the ticket is booked, and confirmed the day before the flight.

Facilities for getting disabled or elderly passengers on or off aircraft vary with different airports. At Heathrow, for instance, the airport authority can provide an ambulance across the airfield and two men to carry the person on or off the plane. The airline is charged for this service. Some airlines absorb this cost in their overheads but others charge the individual passenger. This can add quite considerably to the cost of travelling. It is wise to check first.

The British Airports Authority has produced a leaflet for disabled travellers called *Who looks after you at Heathrow airport?* and similar leaflets for each of its other airports: Gatwick, Stansted, Glasgow, Aberdeen, Prestwick and Edinburgh. Copies of the leaflets are available from the BAA at 2 Buckingham Gate, London SW 1E 6JL, and at the airports.

Most airlines do not charge for carrying a folding wheelchair for someone who is dependent on it. The airline should be told about the wheelchair when the reservation is made and the arrangements should be confirmed before the flight.

The airline's doctor may want to check with the passenger's doctor about the degree of disability and any special attention that might be needed during the flight before accepting a disabled passenger for the flight. It is wise to find out from the airline a few weeks before the intended journey whether medical clearance will be required. The Air Corporations Joint Medical Service, Heathrow, has a booklet *Carriage of invalids by air* giving information about the effect of flying on certain physical conditions, with a medical certificate of fitness for air travel which the passenger's doctor may be asked to complete.

Seats in aircraft are very close together, which makes it difficult to get into a seat and to get up from it. The narrow aisles can also produce problems. It may be necessary for a disabled person to travel 1st class where the seats are farther apart. Seats facing a bulkhead often have more leg room. Some aircraft have a few rear-facing seats which have more space between them and the row facing them.

The lavatories on an aircraft may be inaccessible to a non-ambulant person. Women may find this a major problem, especially on a long journey; a man may be able to manage by using a urinal bottle. For someone who can manage to walk a little, the airline should be asked to reserve a seat near to the lavatory.

Cruises

A small number of passenger ships have a few cabins which are suitable for disabled people. Any disabled or elderly person who hopes to travel by ship should check carefully whether lavatories and bath-rooms, the dining room and other parts of the ship, will be accessible. Even in a ship that has adequate lifts between the various levels, there are other hazards, such as high ledges inside doors and very narrow cabin doors. Cunard will provide details of provision for disabled passengers on their ships; P & O will lend disabled passengers a wheelchair suitable for use on their ships.

Trains

At a large railway station, it may be necessary to do a lot of walking to and from the train but it is usually possible to arrange for a wheelchair to be available, and someone to push it, by giving advance notice to the station manager. British Rail can provide a wheelchair narrow enough to take a passenger to his seat on the train. The Central Council for the Disabled has published *a guide to British Rail* with information about travel arrangements and facilities at major railway stations.

Some of the newer open-plan coaches have sloping handrails and wider doorways which makes access easier. In some, the first table in the coach is removable so that a wheelchair user may be able to remain in his chair throughout the journey. Otherwise, anyone who cannot get out of his wheelchair has to travel in the guard's van. It is advisable to give the station manager two days' notice so that space is kept in the van.

A disabled passenger and accompanying attendant who have to travel in the guard's van can buy tickets at half the second class ordinary single fare for each journey made; if travelling in one of the new first class coaches with space for a wheelchair, only the ordinary second class fare need be paid.

If you can leave your wheelchair for the journey and sit in an ordinary seat, the folded chair is carried free of charge in the brake van provided the chair weighs less than 60lb (27 kg). There is a charge for conveying a non-folding wheelchair.

The exclusive use of a compartment is available on payment of six adult fares.

escort services

The St John Ambulance Brigade will provide an escort to meet or travel with a disabled person who cannot manage alone; a charge is made to cover the travelling expenses. The WRVS also provides an escort service on public transport and to and from local stations. The Red Cross Society's county branches will help and advise disabled people about travelling arrangements within this country, and provide escorts on public transport, or private transport by car or ambulance.

Buses

It is best to travel ouside rush hours or against the stream of commuters. If possible, pick a quiet stop where the bus is likely to pull in close to the kerb. It is also wise to allow extra time for a journey so that you can let a bus go by when conditions are not suitable for boarding. Carrying a stick tends to encourage the bus conductor and other passengers to show more consideration.

Concessionary fares on buses are available in some areas for elderly people, and sometimes for the disabled as well. Concessions range from free travel to cheap rate season tickets. Information on this will be available from the local social services department, or from the public library or the bus company's main office.

Coaches are even more difficult to get on to than buses because of their steep narrow steps. But they usually have the advantage of waiting for a longer time for passengers to get on and off.

Some physiotherapy and occupational therapy departments have replicas of the back section of a bus on which disabled and elderly people can practise. Often a therapist will then go with the person on a short bus ride to help him gain confidence.

H

In most cases, a car with automatic gear change is easier for a disabled person to drive. Several firms will adapt cars for individual disabilities. The British School of Motoring has a Disability Training Centre at 102 Sydney Street, London SW3 6NL, where advice can be obtained on car adaptations, and demonstrations and trial drives in adapted cars arranged. Possible adaptations include all hand-operated controls, all foot-operated controls, or one hand and one leg controls. A disabled candidate applying for a driving test can ask for a priority booking.

There are organisations for disabled drivers: the Disabled Drivers' Association (The Hall, Ashwellthorpe, Norwich NR16 1EX), the Disabled Drivers' Motor Club (39 Templewood, London W13 8DU), the Disabled Motorists' Federation (15 Rookery Road, Tilston, Malpas, Cheshire SY14 7HE).

Getting in and out of a car
Many modern cars have low clearance, which seems even lower when parked alongside a kerb. A four-door car makes access to the back seats easier but a two-door car allows much more room for getting into the front seats.

A disabled or elderly person may find it easiest to get into a car seat backwards, wriggle towards the middle of the car and then lift in the legs. Getting out, first turn and move the back towards the middle of the car, then swing the legs out, making sure that both feet are firmly on the ground before standing up.

There are various rotating car seats that can be fitted to make it easier to get in and out of the car. Some rotate within the car, others rotate and then slide or swing out. Alternatively, a swivelling cushion (made by Rentoul Workshops) may be suitable.

—from a wheelchair
The extra doorway space of a two-door car is useful for an independent wheelchair user for getting the wheelchair into the car. A wheelchair user usually has to get into the car from the passenger side, fold the chair, transfer to the driver's side, and then pull the wheelchair in. A wheelchair can usually be pulled more easily into a car by lifting in the small front wheels first and so gaining leverage for its heavier end.

Someone in a wheelchair may need a board to bridge the gap between the wheelchair and the car seat. A hand grip, in the form of a stirrup handle hooked on to the car roof, may also be needed. This has to be placed in position whenever it is to be used.

Another way of enabling a wheelchair user to travel by car is to adapt a van to take a wheelchair. This may mean raising the roof or lowering the floor, or both, to provide sufficient head room, and providing a tail lift or ramp at the back. It will be necessary to have a means of locking the wheelchair in position to the floor of the van, and providing a seat belt for the person in the chair.

To get a severely disabled person into and out of a car, it may be necessary to use a small mobile hoist. The Burvill hoist can be fixed permanently on to the car. Someone has to work the hoist for the disabled person.

cushions and supports
A disabled person with weakness or paralysis of the lower part of the body may feel uncomfortable when sitting still in a car for a long period, and there is always the danger of pressure sores. Someone who is likely to make long journeys in a car could use one of the anti-pressure cushions designed for wheelchairs.

A back support can be fitted over the back of any car seat or a rally driver's moulded seat installed. Adjustable side pads are available which provide sideways support for the lower spine, and prevent sideways sway. This may be useful for someone with weak trunk muscles.

DHSS and help with outdoor transport
Prior to 1 January 1976, disabled people in certain categories could be supplied by the Department of Health and Social Security under the national health service with an invalid tricycle (a motorised or electric three-wheeler) or a private car allowance towards the cost of running a privately owned adapted car or, in some specific cases, with a small car adapted as necessary by the DHSS. All such vehicles were exempt from road tax (vehicle excise duty), and so was one owned by a person too disabled to drive but in which he could be driven by someone else. People

entitled to help under this invalid vehicle service scheme could continue to receive it regardless of their age for as long as they continued to satisfy the appropriate conditions and criteria.

On 1 January 1976, a cash allowance was introduced to replace the invalid vehicle service scheme for new applicants from that date. This mobility allowance is being introduced gradually by age groups, over a period of about three years, in the broad order of, firstly, those aged 15 to 50, then children 5 to 14 and then people aged 51 to pensionable age (60 for women, 65 for men). Mobility allowance is not paid while any other type of help with outdoor transport is provided under the national health service scheme.

Since 1 January 1976, no adapted cars have been issued and no new private car allowances have been given (except to war disabled pensioners). But someone already in receipt of this type of benefit can continue with it after pensionable age. Since 23 July 1976, a disabled mother with an adapted car supplied by the DHSS because she has a handicapped child will not have the car taken away when the child reaches the age of 14 if the child needs extensive parental care after that age. Also since that date, someone who has had a DHSS adapted car or a three-wheeler or a private car allowance because he needed it to enable him to get to work will not have this taken away when he ceases to be employed.

—mobility allowance

Mobility allowance can at present be claimed by disabled people aged 11 to 50. To qualify, the disabled person must be unable to walk or virtually unable to do so because of physical disablement and likely to remain so for at least 12 months. Assessment may involve a medical examination either at a doctor's surgery (travelling expenses can be claimed) or, if necessary, at home.

Currently (autumn 1976), the mobility allowance is £5 a week and is payable regardless of whether the disabled person can drive or owns a car. It is paid in addition to other social security benefits without adjustment except where a special payment of supplementary benefit is made specifically to meet immobility needs (in such a case, the supplementary benefit payment may be reduced). Mobility allowance is taxable as part of earned income. It is awarded for a specific period of time, at least a year and often up to pensionable age—when it is withdrawn. The disabled person must live in the United Kingdom and have lived in the UK for at least 12 months out of the 18 months preceding his claim for the allowance. Mobility allowance is not paid to anyone who becomes disabled over pensionable age, nor is it paid to someone who is getting an alternative form of help with transport under the NHS scheme.

Leaflet NI 211, available from the Mobility Allowance Unit, North Fylde Central Offices, Norcross, Blackpool FY5 3TA, and from social security offices, DHSS appliance centres and many voluntary organisations, gives details of mobility allowance and incorporates an application form (MY1). Arrangements for war pensioners are different; the relevant leaflet is NI 211A.

—three-wheelers

From 1 January 1976 until 23 July 1976, an invalid tricycle or three-wheeler was available as an alternative to the cash allowance for those who were eligible under the mobility allowance scheme but preferred to have a three-wheeler and were able to drive it. This choice has now been withdrawn: on 23 July, it was announced that invalid three-wheelers would be phased out. None will now be supplied to new applicants under the mobility allowance scheme. But a disabled person between the ages of 51 and 60 (if a woman) or 65 (if a man) who would be eligible for mobility allowance but is in an age group not yet able to receive it, may still be able to have a three-wheeler supplied, provided the criteria (such as being able to drive the vehicle) are met. A three-wheeler issued under this arrangement will be withdrawn when the person reaches pensionable age.

It is proposed to legislate so that people who were supplied with a three-wheeler or private car allowance under the previous invalid vehicle scheme can give up their three-wheeler or allowance and switch instead to a mobility allowance which will continue without upper age limit—provided that they still meet the criteria.

The phasing out of three-wheelers is likely to take up to five years, and possibly longer. New three-wheelers will be manufactured for a year or so for the DHSS but used mainly as replacements for existing users.

Three-wheelers already supplied by the DHSS will continue to be maintained by the Department and replaced free of charge when necessary (unless the need for replacement is due to the driver's negligence) for the next few years while three-wheelers are being phased out.

The appliance centre which supplied the vehicle can be asked for the name and address of the nearest repairer who specialises in repairs to invalid tricycles. Each of the repairers has a large catchment area and if you live in a remote place, the nearest approved repairer may be 50 miles away. The DHSS therefore allow minor and emergency repairs and minor servicing to be done at a local garage. But it is not wise to have work done at a garage which is not familiar with invalid tricycles and does not carry the necessary spares. Minor repairs and servicing are paid for by the DHSS without prior approval, but major repairs have to be approved. This sometimes leads to delays and you can ask the appliance centre for another three-wheeler on temporary loan meantime. Eventually when no more repairs can be carried out, the three-wheeler will be withdrawn and, if possible, replaced. If it cannot be replaced, a mobility allowance may be payable instead.

Parking

Local authorities in England, Scotland and Wales operate an orange badge scheme to help disabled people with some parking problems. Some of the London boroughs have not joined the national scheme and do not therefore recognise the orange badges issued by other local authorities; they operate their own schemes of parking concessions for disabled people who live or work in their areas, and issue orange badges to these people for use elsewhere.

An orange badge exempts the holder from charges and time limits at parking meters, and from time limits when waiting is limited to a specific period; it also allows parking for up to two hours on yellow lines except where there is a ban on loading or unloading in force at the time. It does not entitle the holder to park in bus lanes or 'clearways'. Nor does it exempt the holder from the ban on parking on the zig-zag markings at pedestrian crossings or at the kerbside where there are double white lines in the centre of the road.

Disabled people who have considerable difficulty in walking are entitled to an orange badge, for use when driving or being driven in their own vehicle and when being driven in someone else's. The badge should be displayed behind the windscreen of the vehicle. To park for two hours where there are yellow lines, an additional disc (also orange) is required in England and Wales, to be set to the time of arrival in the parking place; in Scotland, parking on yellow lines is permitted without a time restriction.

An application for an orange badge and time disc should usually be made to the social services department of the local authority; sometimes they are issued by the traffic department. Authorities may charge a fee for the badge but most do not do so. Unless you already have a vehicle supplied by the DHSS or receive a private car allowance, your application should be accompanied by a medical certificate as evidence of your disability. A second 'disabled' badge for display in the car's rear window is also obtainable from the local authority; its use is not compulsory.

A distress pennant for a disabled driver who needs help on the road is available from the Cleveland Spastics Society (The Work Centre, Acklam Road, Middlesbrough, Cleveland TS5 4EG), and a breakdown sticker from the National Federation of St Raphael Clubs (11 Thurlin Road, King's Lynn, Norfolk PE30 4QQ).

Some of the voluntary organisations concerned with disabled or elderly people help with a wide range of problems and others concentrate on those who suffer from one type of major disability or a particular chronic illness. In recent years, there have been moves towards coordinating the work of these bodies, both at national and at local level, to encourage them to pool their resources wherever this is possible and to spend their money in the way that benefits most people in need.

Councils for voluntary service

A council for voluntary service is made up of representatives of organisations concerned with any aspect of community life. It aims to facilitate cooperation between voluntary and statutory bodies in the community, to act as an information centre and to stimulate action to fill gaps in the existing local services. Some councils provide services direct where there is no other appropriate organisation to undertake the work, or on an agency basis for another organisation. Some councils for voluntary service run volunteer bureaux to encourage voluntary work in the community.

The National Council of Social Service (26 Bedford Square, London WC1B 3HU) issues books on many topics, and among its own publications is *Voluntary social services* which lists all kinds of organisations, some charitable, some not, with a brief description of what they do.

Citizens' advice bureaux

Citizens' advice bureaux provide advice and information on any subject. A bureau will, if necessary, take action on behalf of an enquirer or arrange for specialist help from, for example, their legal adviser or a social worker. The bureaux are staffed mainly by volunteers; all CAB workers, unpaid and paid, are trained.

There are about 700 citizens' advice bureaux in the UK. Many are open during normal office hours and perhaps on one or two evenings a week or saturday; others for more restricted hours. Some enquiries can be answered by telephone but for complex problems it is best to go to the bureau; home visits are sometimes possible.

The National Association of Citizens' Advice Bureaux (26 Bedford Square, London WC 1B 3HU) provides bureaux with up-to-date information about legislation, social services, other organisations, and any other relevant material.

The Women's Royal Voluntary Service

The WRVS is a nation-wide service with approximately 1500 offices and branches in Great Britain. The WRVS is responsible for the meals-on-wheels service in many areas of the country. Many branches run clubs and a books-on-wheels service for the housebound of all ages. WRVS members will escort disabled people to and from stations and throughout journeys, and visit housebound people. A WRVS Good Companions scheme provides helpers for people who are finding it difficult to run their own home without assistance: a Good Companion will clean windows, go shopping, do the ironing, and carry out practical jobs around the house, such as changing light bulbs, renewing electric flex and plugs, mowing the lawn or clipping the hedge. In certain areas where there is no public transport, the WRVS, at the request of the local authority, runs a rural social transport scheme to enable elderly and disabled people to visit doctors, chiropodists, relatives in hospital.

The address of a local branch of the WRVS is in the telephone directory or can be obtained from WRVS headquarters, 17 Old Park Lane, London W1Y 4AJ.

The British Red Cross Society

County branches of the Red Cross throughout the country serve the handicapped in a variety of ways, running social clubs and short-stay residential homes, organising group holidays, providing help with transport and care in the home. In some counties, the Red Cross acts as the agent for the local health authority and lends nursing equipment on a short-term basis for use in the home. It has published an illustrated booklet *Homemade aids for handicapped people*.

Addresses of county branches are in local telephone directories or can be obtained from the national headquarters, 9 Grosvenor Crescent, London SW1X 7EJ.

Old people's welfare organisations

Age Concern (the National Old People's Welfare Council) is one of the best known of the voluntary organisations working solely for the welfare of the elderly. It advises government departments on matters of interest to the elderly, and provides training facilities for voluntary workers. It acts as a general information service, and publishes and distributes books and research reports and leaflets. It is the focal point for more than 1100 local organisations providing voluntary services for the elderly.

The address of Age Concern (England) is Bernard Sunley House, 60 Pitcairn Road, Mitcham, Surrey, CR4 3LL.

The numerous voluntary independent organisations for the welfare of elderly people set up by local initiative and interest come under different names, such as senior citizens committee, old people's welfare association, council for the care of the elderly. They vary in size, in the area they cover and the services they provide. Generally, such an organisation acts as a centre of information on local services for the elderly and also usually provides some services. Some organisations extend their work to give help to the relatives of elderly people. The citizens' advice bureau or a council for voluntary service or the local authority social services department should know whether there is an old people's welfare organisation in the area and how to get in contact with it, or Age Concern can be asked.

Youth groups

There are many local organisations of young people who wish to help with some form of voluntary work. Much of their work is concerned with helping the elderly. Because the volunteers are young and active, they often take on tasks that demand hard physical work: springcleaning a house, painting and decorating, tidying up the garden. They may be prepared to climb ladders and deal with inaccessible dirty windows and ceilings—jobs which are outside the range of a home help's work. They will also carry out regular duties such as visiting to keep a housebound person company, doing the shopping, or taking washing to the launderette or laundry.

The citizens' advice bureau or a council for voluntary service will know if there is a youth group, such as Task Force or Community Service Volunteers, in the area, or a local secondary school may offer such a service.

Youth clubs for both the physically handicapped and ablebodied have been formed in many places. The address for information about PHAB clubs and residential courses is 42 Devonshire Street, London W1N 1LN.

Organisations concerned with specific conditions
Some organisations are large and well-known, such as the Spastics Society; others are tiny because relatively few people suffer from the disease, for instance, the Brittle Bone Society. Some organisations have branches throughout the country, others very few. Some concentrate mainly on visiting or providing an information or advisory service, others raise funds to help their members with individual problems and finance the running of clubs or transport or holidays. It is often worthwhile contacting the relevant organisation to find out what it does. Even when help is not required at the moment, there may be a need later and it is useful to know whether the organisation would ever be able to help.

Details of voluntary organisations can be found in reference books in the public library, such as the *Charities Digest* produced annually by the Family Welfare Association (501 Kingsland Road, London E8 4AA) and *Guide to the social services*, also produced by the FWA and revised annually (this is a reference guide for social workers, citizens' advice bureaux and voluntary workers who have some background knowledge). If you have difficulty getting the information you require through the public library, you should contact the local social services department, the CAB or council for voluntary service. The King's Fund Centre (126 Albert Street, London NW1 7NE) produces a list of organisations relating to the health and social services.

There are a number of voluntary organisations (such as the Arthritis and Rheumatism Council for Research, the National Corporation for the Care of Old People, the Joint Committee on Mobility for the Disabled) concerned with fund raising and research or acting as a pressure group for particular aspects of disability. Of the many others which help individuals with information, finance or other practical matters, the following is a selection.

The Central Council for the Disabled (34 Eccleston Square, London SW1V 1PE) issues a monthly information bulletin on current matters of concern to disabled people, and publishes, sponsors and distributes many other publications. It has a legal and parliamentary committee and issues circulars on particular topics, such as rating and taxation. The CCD has done work and gives advice on holiday problems, access for the disabled, mobility, housing and other problems of disability. It also maintains a travelling exhibition of everyday aids for disabled people.

The British Council for Rehabilitation of the Disabled (Tavistock House South, Tavistock Square, London WC1H 9LB) arranges courses and conferences on rehabilitation and disablement and publishes a magazine called *Rehabilitation*. It also operates a preparatory training bureau which is concerned with the education and training of handicapped people with a view to their re-employment. The Council has established rehabilitation engineering movement advisory panels (REMAP).

The Disablement Income Group (Toynbee Hall, 28 Commercial Street, London E1 6LR) aims to improve the financial situation of disabled people, particularly disabled housewives. It runs an advisory service, does research and produces publications, including *An ABC of services and general information for disabled people*. There are about 80 local branches of DIG.

The National Council for the Single Woman and Her Dependants (29 Chilworth Mews, London W2) includes among its activities a pen friend club and a bi-monthly newsletter. The Council has 43 branches throughout the country which hold meetings and organise outings and other activities.

Association of Disabled Professionals (general secretary: Mrs Angela

Croall, Broadwell, Graffham, near Petworth, West Sussex) gives advice to any disabled person who wants to follow a professional career despite a disability. The ADP does not act as an employment agency. It seeks to expand the educational and employment opportunities of all disabled people.

Help the Aged (8 Denman Street, London W1A 2AP), among its activities for old people, promotes sheltered housing schemes, day centres and good neighbour schemes. It publishes a monthly newspaper, *Yours,* and commissions and publishes special reports.

Invalids-at-home (secretary: Mrs J Pierce, 23 Farm Avenue, London NW2 2BJ) aims to help permanent invalids to leave hospital for home by making grants or interest-free loans for additional heavy expenditure or by providing special equipment to ensure their safety and comfort.

British Limbless Ex-Service Men's Association (Frankland Moore House, 185/7 High Road, Chadwell Heath, Essex RM6 6NA) assists and advises on matters concerning pensions, allowances and welfare. There are branches throughout the country, and two Blesma homes for permanent and temporary residents.

The Spastics Society (12 Park Crescent, London W1N 4EQ) organises a mobile exhibition of aids for the disabled, and publishes and distributes reports and booklets of interest to the disabled, including a series of parents' handbooks. The Society provides supportive services, schools and centres for people of all ages, and finances research.

The Chest and Heart Association (Tavistock House North, Tavistock Square, London WC1H 9JE) helps those suffering from a heart condition, asthma, chronic bronchitis or other chest condition. It organises clubs throughout the country for stroke sufferers, where people with speech problems may be helped to overcome their difficulties and regain the ability to communicate with others. The CHA provides a counselling service, and produces leaflets and other publications about chest and heart illnesses, including *Return to independence* to help stroke patients regain mobility.

British Rheumatism and Arthritis Association (1 Devonshire Place, London W1N 2BD) gives information and advice on individual problems and has a network of local branches throughout the country. The BRA maintains five holiday hotels, a residential home for the severely disabled and a block of residential flatlets, and supplies aids for the disabled which can be seen and tried out at the London headquarters (there is a leaflet describing the aids that are available). The BRA *Review* is published quarterly.

Parkinson's Disease Society (81 Queens Road, London SW19 8NR) runs an information and advisory service for sufferers from parkinsonism and their families to help with problems which arise in the home, and publishes booklets and other informative literature, and a news letter. It also raises money to sponsor research.

The Multiple Sclerosis Society (4 Tachbrook Street, London SW1V 1SJ) encourages research into multiple sclerosis, and offers an advice and welfare service. There are branches throughout the country.

Action for Research into Multiple Sclerosis (71 Grays Inn Road, London WC1X 8TR) runs a telephone counselling service to give help, advice or just a friendly ear for all who suffer from multiple sclerosis and for those near to them. The service is available 24 hours a day, 7 days a week and is manned by counsellors who know about multiple sclerosis from personal experience. The telephone number is 01-568 2255.

Muscular Dystrophy Group (Nattrass House, 35 Macaulay Road, London SW4 0QP) raises funds for research into muscular dystrophy and allied neuromuscular diseases and helps sufferers and those who care for them, wherever possible using existing statutory and voluntary bodies. It publishes a quarterly newspaper, information leaflets, and a practical guide *The muscular dystrophy handbook*. There are local branches.

The British Polio Fellowship (Bell Close, West End Road, Ruislip, Middlesex, HA4 6LP) aims to help polio victims in their rehabilitation. It provides a personal welfare service to help with finance or advice, runs hostels and provides holiday accommodation, promotes physical exercise in the form of an annual sports, swimming and indoor games competition.

Spinal Injuries Association (general secretary: Miss Diana Irish, 126 Albert Road, London NW1 7NE) promotes the interests of people who have been paralysed by a spinal cord injury. It has published the book *So you're paralysed*.

Friedreich's Ataxia Group (Bolsover House, 5/6 Clipstone Street, London W1) supports research into the cause of the disease and provides advice and assistance to sufferers and their families.

Greater London Association for the Disabled (183 Queensway, London W2 5HL) is the central body for London borough associations. GLAD gives advice and information on all aspects of welfare for the disabled in Greater London, and has a directory of clubs for the handicapped. It produces a journal, *Glad News*, and occasional publications.

The National Federation of St Raphael Clubs (11 Thurlin Road, King's Lynn, Norfolk PE30 4QQ) acts as the coordinator of St Raphael clubs for the disabled throughout mainly the eastern counties of England and keeps them informed of the services available to all disabled people. It arranges holidays for disabled people and their relatives.

How others can help

Social workers and local authorities are often criticised because so many elderly or disabled people are left lonely. A friendly neighbour may be able to do more than a harassed social worker who cannot spare the time just for talk. There are many people who could spend some time helping to look after a disabled or elderly person but who do not know whom to contact or are unsure whether they have anything to offer. A would-be volunteer may find it helpful to read *A guide to voluntary service* published by Her Majesty's Stationery Office.

Volunteer bureaux have been established in many parts of the country, some with help from the local authority, to develop and make better use of the services of volunteers in the community. Many people interested in voluntary service need some preliminary advice and discussion before approaching any particular statutory or voluntary agency. This can help to avoid the frustration and discouragement of potential volunteers due to a lack of specific information about local needs for voluntary help. Volunteer bureaux provide an information service for prospective volunteers and act as a central recruiting agency to put local organisations and volunteers in touch with each other. The Volunteer Centre (29 Lower King's Road, Berkhamsted, Herts HP4 2AB) keeps a register of volunteer bureaux and can be asked for information.

Good neighbour schemes have started up in many parts of the country. They are organised in a variety of ways, offer different kinds of help and go under different names, such as community link, community care groups, 'fish' schemes. A local council for voluntary service or a volunteer bureau will know whether there is such a scheme in the area.

The help that is given by good neighbours can cover almost anything. It may consist mainly of visiting and talking and listening. It may mean going shopping or exercising the dog. It may mean going into the house every morning to help a disabled person dress and returning in the evening to put her to bed. Running a car pool can be another useful service, to take housebound people to the optician, to the dentist, to visit a relative in hospital, to the shops to buy new clothes. Sitting with an old person is another way to help, so that the relatives can go out for an evening or the day or even occasionally stay away for the night. The main thing good neighbour schemes have in common is that they are designed to use the resources of some members of the community to meet the particular needs of others.

INDEX

Care of the feet

describes the foot, its structure and growth, and gives advice on looking after your feet, including for those who are elderly or at risk. It discusses the importance of finding suitable shoes that fit properly and goes in detail through common foot troubles, their probable cause and the treatment available from doctor or chiropodist to alleviate pain and discomfort caused, for example, by corns and callosities, bunion joints, hammer toes. The book also deals with general disorders of the body that affect the feet, such as osteoarthrosis, gout, rheumatoid arthritis, and the provision of surgical or adapted shoes when required for deformed feet.

Avoiding back trouble

explains how the spine is constructed and how not to stress it in everyday activities such as housework, driving, lifting and carrying, gardening, sitting. It describes symptoms of back trouble and advises on how to cope with an acute attack of back pain. It tells what to expect when examined by specialists (including the diagnostic terms that may be used) and the treatments that may be prescribed, whether just staying in bed, wearing a corset, having physiotherapy, surgery, or one of the many manipulative techniques. The book ends with suggestions about how to avoid becoming a chronic back sufferer.

Caring for teeth

tells people how to look after their teeth. There is advice about diet and oral hygiene, and a section about the profession describes the general dental service, private dentistry and ancillary help. Other chapters describe dental and periodontal diseases and the treatment available, false teeth and how to look after them, and what to do and where to go in an emergency.

Treatment and care in mental illness

deals briefly with the illnesses concerned and describes the help available through the national health service, from the local authority and from voluntary organisations. It explains the medical treatment a mentally ill person receives as an outpatient or an inpatient, and deals with community care and aftercare. It includes a chapter on the symptoms and treatment of mental illness in old age.

Eyes right
explains how the eyes work, and describes in detail various eye diseases and complaints, including glaucoma and cataract, and gives advice on seeking treatment through the national health service or privately. Changes in eyesight in middle and old age are specifically dealt with.

Pregnancy month by month
tells in detail what can be expected at every stage of antenatal care. The book discusses the choice of where to have a baby and compares the advantages of hospital, g.p. maternity unit, nursing home and home confinement. It gives reasons for the various tests and examinations at antenatal clinics, and considers the effects of drugs and food supplements on a pregnant woman and how to deal with the minor ailments that often accompany pregnancy. The book also covers genetic counselling, contraception, abortion and provisions for unmarried mothers.

Extending your house
describes what is involved in having an extension built on to a house or bungalow. The book is a step by step account of what has to be done, when and by whom. It deals with drawing a sketch plan, consulting an architect or other professional consultant, contacting a builder, arranging a contract and getting quotations. It explains how the Building Regulations affect the position and design of an extension, and how to apply to the local authority for planning permission and Building Regulations approval. For the technically minded, various aspects of construction work are described. There is a glossary and many explanatory drawings.

The legal side of buying a house
goes through the procedure on the typical transfer of a house in England or Wales (but not Scotland) which is wholly occupied by the seller and has a registered title. It contains a detailed description of what has to be done, and the parts played by the solicitors, the estate agent, the surveyor, the Land Registry, the insurance company and the local authority. The book also deals with the somewhat less complicated business of the legal side of selling a house.

Wills and probate
is a book about wills and why and how to make them, and about the administration of an estate by executors without the help of a solicitor. It explains clearly about reading the will, the valuation of the estate, what is involved in obtaining probate, payment of capital transfer tax, and the distribution of the estate. It also shows, with examples, how to prepare a will, sign it, and have it witnessed.

Central heating
helps you to choose central heating for your home, telling you how to find a good installer to carry out the work and giving details of the equipment involved—boilers, radiators, convectors and other heat emitters, thermostats and other controls, warm air units and ducting. It discusses the merits of the different fuels and helps you assess their relative running costs, and highlights the importance of improving insulation. One section deals with problems that may arise after installation and advises on avoiding hazards.

Living through middle age
faces up to the changes that this stage of life may bring, whether inevitable (in skin, hair, eyes, teeth) or avoidable, such as being overweight, smoking or drinking too much, insomnia. It discusses the symptoms and treatment of specific disorders that are fairly common in men and women over 40, and for women the effects of the menopause and gynaecological problems. Psychological difficulties for both men and women are discussed, and the possible need for sexual adjustment. Throughout, practical advice is given on overcoming problems that may arise so that you can make the most of your middle years.

Outings and in-things for children
A handbook for parents who would like help in keeping their five-to-twelve year old children occupied out of school-hours, including zoos and museums. It is a source-book of how to get hold of more information, much of it free. There are sections on sports and outdoor activities, clubs, town-trails, farm-trails, and visits to prehistoric sites, bird-watching, keeping pets and suggestions for rainy afternoons at home.

Health for old age
is written in layman's language to help older people to understand and cope with the difficulties and illnesses that may arise with advancing years. The book advises generally on maintaining health and talks sensibly about such afflictions as arthritis, thrombosis, constipation, failing sight and hearing, heart failure. Symptoms to report to the doctor are discussed, and remedies available.

Having an operation
describes the procedure for admission to hospital and tells you what happens there: ward routine, hospital personnel, preparation for the operation, anaesthesia, post-operative treatment and recovery, arrangements for discharge, and convalescence. Basic information is given about some of the more common operations.

other Consumer Publications include:
- **What to do when someone dies**
- **Claiming on home, car and holiday insurance**
- **How to sue in the county court**
- **Owning a car**
- **Infertility**
- **The newborn baby**
- **How to adopt**
- **Electricity supply and safety**
- **Getting a divorce**
- **Dismissal, redundancy and job hunting**

CONSUMER PUBLICATIONS are available from Consumers' Association, Caxton Hill, Hertford SG 13 7LZ, and from booksellers.

...and for the medical profession

the *Drug and Therapeutics Bulletin,* published fortnightly, helps prescribers to keep up to date with developments in drug therapy: named drugs are assessed and the latest research on effects, side-effects and the therapeutic use are concisely assessed. The *Drug and Therapeutics Bulletin* is independent of manufacturers and carries no advertisements; it can be read in a few minutes. Subscription details are available from the Consumers' Association.